Anonymous

Short Instructive Sketches From the Lives of the Saints

Anonymous

Short Instructive Sketches From the Lives of the Saints

ISBN/EAN: 9783337340308

Printed in Europe, USA, Canada, Australia, Japan

Cover: Foto ©Lupo / pixelio.de

More available books at **www.hansebooks.com**

nstructive Sketches

FROM THE

J. SCHAEFER, PUBLISHER, 60 BARCLAY STREET,

1888.

PREFACE.

Ours is the great age of reading, and no small portion of the literature of our day is made up of light, amusing, stirring matter, calculated to delight the fancy, and tickle the imagination, as a pastime. It is in great measure an everyday literature, like the one-day flies, yet if this were the only purpose of so many publications, we need not sound the cry of alarm. But, alas! what a deluge of trashy literature, immoral in tendency and irreligious in principle, is placed upon the market, which poisons the mind, corrupts the heart of our youths, whereby full sway is given to the well-known spiritual enemies described by the Apostle St. John. We must, therefore, welcome any really good book to offset these treacherous shoots of vile bookmaking.

Of what importance and influence good or bad examples are upon the children and youths of our period need not be stated again. Those who can boast of the advantages of education in the so-called higher classes of society are growing looser in their habits of Christian life, weaker in the teachings of divine truth, while piety and faith seem rather to be flourishing among the poor and humble, who have before them the model lives and example of virtuous parents having at heart to place good reading on the family table and at the fireside of their homes.

To aid somewhat the holy cause of spreading good books with a view of opposing the evil current of bad literature, and counteracting the sad ravages of mere worldly heroes, the publisher places this little book, entitled, "*Short Sketches from the Lives of the Saints*," before a Christian community. It is intended to lay down, in pithy and concise chapters, suitable to youthful minds, the bright examples of God's chosen Saints, now in the enjoyment of immortal bliss. This small volume shall fix your eyes, my dear young readers, upon these illustrious guides in your own daily walks of life, that you may copy them, and thus taste of the pleasure and delight of serving God on earth.

This small *vade mecum* may serve as a stepping-stone to the larger "Lives of the Saints," with which you, my young friends, I hope, may yet become familiar. That the reading of these "Sketches" may produce such result is the sincere wish of

THE PUBLISHER.

CONTENTS.

	PAGE
Agatha, St., Martyrdom of	7
Agatho, The Hermit, and his Pupils	65
Agnes, St., Martyrdom of	6
Alfonsus Liguori, St	183
Aloysius Gonzaga, St.:	
His Birth and Vocation	157
His Mortifications	161
His Death	162
Amadeus, Duke, The Hounds of	100
American Saints Recently Placed in the Proper for the United States	194
Anglo-Saxons Received Christianity, How the	67
Anthony of Padua, St.:	
The Saint's Sermon	101
How the Creature Revered the Creator	102
The Saint Preaches to the Fishes	103
The Saint and the Child Jesus	104
The Saint's Tongue	105
Arbogast, St., Restores a King's Son to Life	59
Arius, a Judgment of God on	34
Augustine, St	49
Beasts of the Forest Obey a Saint	96
Bernard, St., A Miracle by	92

CONTENTS.

	PAGE
Bernardine of Sienna, St.:	
As a Youth	127
As a Preacher	128
Benedict, St.:	
How he Rescued his Pupil, Maurus	53
Totila and St. Benedict	54
Bishop before a Judge, A	35
Blasius, St.:	
Miracle of	24
Death of	24
Boniface, St.:	
The Saint and the Ancient Oak	73
Martyrdom of the Saint	74
Bridget, St., the Choice of	72
Cassian, St., Death of	11
Catharine of Sienna, St., and Pope Gregory XIII.	126
Catharine, St., Death of	8
Charlemagne and Bishop Ludgerus	75
Charles Borromeo, St.	171
Christian Martyrs in the Arena	1
Christophorus, St., Legend of	42
Clara, Mother:	
How she Multiplied the Half-loaf	99
Puts a Horde of Warriors to Flight	99
Conrad, Bishop:	
His Reverence for the Holy Sacrament	83
His Gift of Prophecy	83
Constantine the First Christian Emperor	31
Corpus Christi, The Origin of	99
Crispin and Crispinian, SS., Martyrs	16

CONTENTS.

	PAGE
Cross, Power of the Sign of the	51
Cunigunde, Empress, Canonization of	87
Cuthbert, St.:	
How he Ruled Wind and Fire	63
How God Provided him and his Pupil with Food	64
Cyprian, St., Death of	10
Death of St. Kilian	68
Death of St. Patrick	40
Dominic, St :	
A Miracle by	112
Another Miracle by	113
Origin of the Rosary	114
Early Christians in the Catacombs, The	2
Edward the Confessor, St.	132
Elegius, St., Honesty of	62
Elizabeth, St.:	
How she Became Landgravine	106
Her Roses	107
How she Became a Widow	108
Sufferings and Death of	109
Canonization of	111
Ephraim, St., Patience of	45
Felix of Cantalicio, St., and the Judge	170
Felix, St., and the Spider's Web	25
Fidelis, St., Labors of and Martyrdom in Granbuenden	166
Forty Holy Martyrs, Death of	22
Francis Solan, Heroism of	178, 196

CONTENTS.

PAGE

Francis of Borgia, St.:
 Why he Became a Jesuit...................... 173
 Humility of.. 175
 His Patience...................................... 176
Francis of Paula, St.:
 Louis XI. and the Saint...................... 139
 The Saint Commands the Elements........... 141
Francis, St.:
 In Presence of Sultan Saladin................ 115
 The Saint and the Poor...................... 116
 The Christmas Crib 117
Francis Xavier, St.:
 His Labors....................................... 148
 His Miracles.................................... 150

Galuzzi, Father, and the Criminals.............. 94
Genevieve, St..................................... 56
Gualbert, St...................................... 88

How Agatho Taught Conscientiousness.......... 65
Huns before Paris, and St. Genevieve........... 56
Hugo, St., and the Cavalier..................... 84

Ignatius of Loyola................................ 146
Ignatius, Patriarch, and the Schismatic Photius. 76
Isidore, St., a Peasant........................... 61

John of Capistrano, St.:
 The Saint and the Hussites.................... 134
 His Power Over the Elements................. 135
 The Courageous Monk......................... 136

CONTENTS.

	PAGE
John of Kanti, St., Simplicity of	124
John of Matha, St.	130
Jordan, The Blessed, Generosity of	145
Judgment of God, A	34
Kilian, St., and Companions, Martyrdom of	68
Lawrence, St., Death of	12
Leo the Great and Genseric	55
Leo the Iconoclast	36
Lives of Saints Canonized by Leo XIII.:	
Benedict Joseph Labre, St.	190
Clare of Montefalco, St.	183
John Baptist de Rossi, St.	192
Lawrence of Brindisi, St.	188
Louis, St., King of France:	
Vows to Undertake a Crusade	118
Chivalrous Act of the Saint	119
Death of St. Louis	121
Martin, St.:	
The Beggar and St. Martin	28
Discharge from the Roman Army	28
Miracle by	30
Mary, Help of Christians	167
Monica, St., The Maternal Love of	47
Nicephorus and Leo the Iconoclast	36
Nicholas, St.	25
Nicholas of the Flüe Insured Peace, How	142
Norbert, St., and his Gatekeeper	91
Notburga, St., a Servant	122

CONTENTS.

	PAGE
Odilo, The Charitable Abbot	66
Ottilia, St., and the Leper	71

Patrick, St.:
    How St. Dorian Saved his Life............ 38
    Death of.................................. 40
Paulinus, St., as a Slave..................... 57
Persecutions under Nero...................... 4
Peter Canisius, The Blessed.................. 164
Peter Claver, St., the Friend of the Negroes.. 180
Peter the Hermit Preaching the Crusades...... 90
Philip Neri, St.:
    The Saint and the Student................ 176
    A Friend of Children..................... 177
Philip of Jesus, St.......................... 194
Phokus, St., Martyrdom of.................... 91

Releasing the Captives....................... 130
Roman, the Holy Abbot, Miracle by............ 41
Rosary, Origin of the........................ 114
Rose of Lima, St............................. 169

Sebastian, St., Martyrdom of................. 2
Sisters of Charity, Founding of the Order of. 182
Spider's Web a Defensive Wall, The........... 25
Spiridion, Bishop, How he Converted Arians... 32
Stanislaus Kostka, St........................ 152

Teresa of Jesus, St.......................... 154
Theban Legion, Martyrdom of the.............. 21
Theodosius and Archbishop Ambrose............ 50

CONTENTS.

PAGE

Thomas of Villanova, St. :
   His Charity when a Child..................... 143
   As Archbishop 144
Timotheus and Maura, SS., Martyrs............ 15
Thomas Aquinas, St., Piety of.................. 131
Trudbert, St., in the Black Forest,.............. 69
Turribius, St., Archbishop of Lima.............. 195

Ulrich, Holy Bishop, Miracle by................. 78

Valentin, St., Martyr........................... 13
Vincent de Paul, St............................. 182
Vitus, St., Martyr.............................. 17

Wenceslaus of Bohemia, St. :
   Humility of..................................... 85
   Martyrdom of.................................. 86
We should Forgive those who Injure Us......... 88
Wolfgang, Bishop :
   His Magnanimity to a Beggar................... 79
   His Death...................................... 80

THE CHRISTIAN MARTYRS IN THE ARENA.

THE Roman amphitheatres consisted of large oval or circular buildings, with rows of seats, one above another, around an open space, which they called the "arena." Below these rows of seats there were cages and stalls for ferocious beasts, such as lions, tigers, leopards, bulls, etc. On certain days thousands of people would occupy the seats around the arena for the purpose of witnessing a cruel spectacle. Slaves were placed in the arena to fight with each other; or, what happened more frequently and was wildly applauded by the heathen spectators, one of the wild animals was let loose and the slave had to fight for his life, but generally fell a prey to the hungry wild beast. When the emperors began to persecute the early Christians, they substituted the latter for the slaves. The cruel beasts would spring on them, tear and devour them, leaving nothing but the harder bones. When the cruel spectacle was over and the amphitheatre empty, some Christians would gather the remains of the victims to preserve them piously as precious relics.

THE EARLY CHRISTIANS IN THE CATACOMBS.

The early Christians had to suffer terrible persecutions in almost every part of the vast Roman Empire. Especially in the city of Rome, the residence of the emperor, the Christians were tortured and murdered without mercy. In their trouble they took refuge in the catacombs, which they made their temporary homes. These catacombs were mines, with caverns, grottoes and gangways, extending in the tufa layers under a considerable part of the city of Rome. In those gangways they dug receptacles on the right and left side, one above another, in which the remains of the saints and martyrs were buried; the open side of the graves they covered with large stones, on which they engraved religious emblems, with the names of the martyrs. In these subterranean caverns the Christians assembled to attend Catholic service. Even there, below the surface of the earth, the Christians were in constant danger. It often happened that when leaving the hidden asylum they were seized and imprisoned. Many times they were shut up in the catacombs, buried alive and starved. The Emperor Constantine discontinued the persecution, granting peace and religious liberty to the Christians.

THE PERSECUTION UNDER THE EMPEROR NERO.

ONE of the worst persecutors of the Christians was the Emperor Nero. After having wallowed in all vices, he had the city of Rome fired in order to present a representation of the burning of Troy. He witnessed the fire from the summit of a tall tower; it lasted for eight days, and almost destroyed the entire city. When the tyrant heard that the people suspected him of being the author of the conflagration, he endeavored to throw the blame on the Christians. The populace did not believe him; but they seized the occasion to persecute the hated Christians. The Christians were therefore denounced to the authorities, sought out, imprisoned, thrown to the wild beasts, beheaded, cast into caldrons of boiling oil, covered with pitch and attached to posts, when they were burned alive, and used to light either the emperor's garden or the public plazas. During this terrible persecution Saints Peter and Paul suffered martyrdom.

MARTYRDOM OF ST. SEBASTIAN.

St. Sebastian was a colonel in the Roman army. When the Emperor Maximian learned that he, Sebastian, had become a Christian, he was turned over to the bowmen. He was tied by them to a tree and left for dead, after having been pierced by arrows. Irena, the widow of a martyr, reverently made arrangements to bury the body. When she found life was not extinct, she had him transferred to her house, where he recovered. Zealous of suffering martyrdom for Christ, Sebastian appeared before Maximian and represented the injustice of the persecution of the Christians. The emperor grew furious, and had Sebastian dragged to a public place and beaten to death. His saintly remains were thrown into a ditch. A Christian widow, named Lucina, had them taken out and buried in the catacombs. Sebastian is represented bound to a tree and shot to death with arrows.

MARTYRDOM OF ST. AGNES.

The holy virgin and martyr St. Agnes was condemned to be burned by the judge, Aspasius. But the flames had no effect on her. The judge thereupon ordered an officer to pierce her neck with a sword. When this was done the saint fell to the earth. The blood gushed from the gaping wound, and she died immediately. Eight days afterward, while her parents were praying at her grave, St. Agnes appeared to them bearing a white lamb in her arms. In remembrance of this, every year two lambs are blessed in her church in Rome, from the wool of which the palliums of the archbishops are made.

MARTYRDOM OF ST. AGATHA.

THE holy virgin and martyr Agatha lived in the Island of Sicily during the persecution of the Christians by the Emperor Decius. The governor, Quintianus, heard of her beauty and wealth, and had her summoned before him. When he could not by persuasion or threats compel her to worship the gods, he had her put to the torture and struck in the face. She was then bound to a pillar, brutally maimed, and subsequently cast into prison. The following night she was wholly healed by an aged man who appeared to her. Filled with rage at seeing her recovered, the governor had her tortured by fire and by rolling her on broken glass till she died. The Church celebrates her feast every year on the 6th of February. She is represented in youthful garb, with a pincers in her hand.

DEATH OF ST. CATHARINE.

The Roman emperor Maximus came to Alexandria while passing through the provinces of his empire. Here he offered solemn sacrifice to the idols. The Christian virgin Catharine, the daughter of distinguished and rich parents, placed herself before the door of the temple and waited for his appearance. When he came out she explained to him his blindness in offering homage to false gods. He was astonished at her courage, and the clearness of her argument, and therefore invited her into his palace, where he assembled the most learned men, in order to dispute with Catharine about religion, and vanquish her. The philosophers sought to bring forward the most important reasons for their idolatry. But Catharine spoke in such a convincing manner of the foolishness of their customs and of the sublimity of the Christian religion, that the whole assemblage of learned men, filled with astonishment, proclaimed themselves Christians. Enraged at this victory of the virgin, Maximus had the philosophers burnt. Then he tried to persuade Catharine, with flatteries and promises, to offer sacrifice to the idols. As he found his enticements fruitless, he caused her to be terribly scourged and thrown into prison. Then he ordered nails to be driven into the felloes of wheels, and Catharine to be tied to them. As the executioners were about to roll them, they broke. The heathens, standing around, then exclaimed: "Great is the Christian's God!" At this sight even the empress could not be prevented from proclaiming herself a Christian. The emperor then had Catharine and the empress beheaded.

DEATH OF ST. CYPRIAN.

DURING the persecution of the Christians by the Emperor Valerian, St. Cyprian, Bishop of Carthage, was seized and dragged before the governor, Galerius Maximus, who, seating himself upon his tribunal, asked him: "Art thou Cyprian, the bishop of the Christians who despise the gods?" The bishop answered: "It is so." The governor then said: "According to the orders of the illustrious emperor, you must offer sacrifice to the gods." Cyprian replied: "I shall never do so." The governor cried: "Consider the consequences of your refusal!" But Cyprian answered: "In such a just cause there is nothing to consider or overlook." Then he was condemned to death by the sword as an enemy of the gods. When he arrived at the place of execution, he knelt down and prayed, then he arose, took off his upper garment, bandaged his eyes himself, and received the deathblow, on the 14th September, 258.

DEATH OF ST. CASSIAN.

ST. CASSIAN was a bishop, and lived in the third century. At Imola he instructed the heathen boys in the ancient languages. But during the instructions he instilled into their hearts the doctrines of Christianity. When this became known in the city, he was accused of propagating a new religion. To the question of the governor as to his occupation or business, Cassian answered: "I proclaim Jesus Christ, the Saviour of the world, to the ignorant." Then the governor attempted to make him forsake his faith. But as he saw that his efforts were in vain, he had the saint stripped and tied to a pillar; he then induced the schoolboys to torture him. Some beat him with their slates, others stuck their pencils into his flesh, and again others went so far in their wantonness as to scratch whole words in his skin. Bleeding from many wounds, the saint expired under the hands of his torturers.

DEATH OF ST. LAWRENCE.

ST. LAWRENCE was a deacon of Pope Sixtus. At the same time he had charge of the Church property, and he had to supervise the distribution of alms to the poor. When the heathens led the Pope away to crucify him, Lawrence said to him: "Father, where goest thou without thy son?" Sixtus answered: "My son, in three days thou wilt follow me." When Lawrence had heard this prophecy, he sold all the valuables in his trust and distributed the proceeds among the poor. The heathen judge then sent for him and demanded the surrender of the property. In answer to this, Lawrence said: "I am ready to obey you." He then went out and brought all the Christian poor before the judge. Incensed at this, the avaricious man commanded Lawrence to deny Jesus Christ, and sought to force him by torture to do so. As this was useless, he had him laid on a red hot iron. When Lawrence had been lying for some time on it, he said to the judge: "You might let me be turned on the other side now, as I am roasted enough on this." After the executioners had turned him several times, to increase his sufferings, he expired.

The Christians gathered his relics, and afterwards they built a church in his honor outside of the walls of Rome, in which his relics are preserved. The Church celebrates his feast on the 10th of August.

ST. VALENTIN, MARTYR.

ST. VALENTIN was a priest of the early Christian congregation at Rome. Under the Emperor Claudius he was seized and put into prison. When he was tried by the judge, Asterius, Valentin said: "Your gods are made of wood or stone, but Christ is the light of the world." Whereupon the judge answered: "I have an adopted daughter who has been blind for the past two years; if you will be able to restore her sight, I also shall believe in Christ." Valentin fell on his knees and prayed: "Lord Jesus Christ, true light, enlighten Thy servant." Scarcely had he uttered these words when the girl opened her eyes and saw. Asterius and his wife, filled with astonishment, fell at the feet of the saint and asked what they should do. The saint commanded them to destroy all their idols. Then he instructed them and baptized them, with all the members of their family. When this event reached the ear of the emperor, he had Valentin, with his new converts, cast into prison, and later they were beheaded, thus gaining the crown of martyrdom.

TIMOTHEUS AND MAURA, MARTYRS.

At the time of the persecution by the Emperor Diocletian, a man named Timotheus and his wife, Maura, living in Egypt, were sentenced to be crucified. When both were brought to the place of execution, Maura's mother hurried to the side of her daughter, and embracing her, cried: "My daughter, wilt thou leave thy mother thus? What shall become of your jewels, your money, your gold and silver, and all your property, when you are dead?" Maura replied: "Dear mother, our gold will be destroyed; moths will eat our clothes; beauty of body shall pass away with time; but the crown of Jesus Christ endures for all eternity!" Saying these words, she freed herself from her mother's embrace, walked to the cross, and was crucified with her husband.

SS. CRISPIN AND CRISPINIAN, MARTYRS.

The Roman youths Crispin and Crispinian were brothers and Christians. About the middle of the third century they traveled to Gaul in order to spread the light of the true faith. Both brothers were shoemakers, and soon acquired an extended reputation on account of their industry and good work. By their frugality they were able to bestow great benefits on the poor. They not only without charge made shoes for the poor, but even furnished them with the leather. The people soon frequented the establishment of the two brothers. They were delighted at their great wisdom, and on the occasion of their meeting sought to learn the divine doctrines. It soon came to pass that many persons had embraced the faith. When the idolatrous priests saw how their temples were being abandoned, they complained of the two brothers to the Roman governor. He sought by promises of pardon and threats to compel them to renounce the Christian faith. As he could not accomplish his purpose, he had them scourged, their backs cut with stripes, and shoemaker-awls thrust under their nails. Then the saints were cast into a caldron of boiling lead. When, however, they emerged unhurt from the caldron, they were beheaded, and their bodies cast to the wild beasts. These saints are the patrons of the shoemaking craft, whose banner for centuries has borne their pictures.

ST. VITUS, MARTYR.

The Roman emperor Diocletian had a daughter who was possessed by an evil spirit. The devil proclaimed that he would not leave her until ordered to do so by St. Vitus. When the fiend was asked where the saint was, he made it known. Whereupon Diocletian had the youth summoned before him, and commanded him to heal his daughter. Vitus then imposed hands on her, marked her with the sign of the cross, and commanded the demon, in the name of Jesus Christ, to depart from the maiden. The demon left her, amid frightful blasphemies. The emperor was astounded, but still would not become a Christian, and sought to induce, by all all sorts of promises, Vitus to abjure his religion. When he saw that his efforts were in vain, he ordered Vitus to be thrown to the lions. But the ferocious animals crept up harmlessly to the feet of the saint. Diocletian ascribed this to witchcraft, and had the saint cast into a caldron of boiling oil. St. Vitus is represented as a boy, with a caldron of boiling oil near him. He is especially invoked in epilepsy.

MARTYRDOM OF ST. PHOKAS.

St. Phokas was a gardener in Sinope. His little garden before the gate of the city, which he cultivated with untiring care, brought him so much, that he could not only live himself, but greatly help the poor. Because he was a disciple of Jesus, he did not escape the notice of the persecutors. As soon as he was reported to the authorities, soldiers were dispatched to his residence, with commands, not to bring him before the authorities, but at once to kill him. On arriving at Sinope, in the evening, worn out, they unknowingly stopped at the door of Phokas, and asked for refreshments. He placed before them a welcome repast and invited them to remain for the night. His benevolence and kindness touched the hearts of the soldiers, so that they confessed they had been sent to seize Phokas in order to murder him. They asked his advice in the matter. Phokas had now a full opportunity to flee, but he was ready to die for Christ. He said to the soldiers: "I know this Phokas. Grant me one day's time, and I shall deliver him up to you." The soldiers gladly waited, and Phokas meantime gave all the necessary orders for his funeral. On the morning of the second day he appeared before the soldiers and said: "I am Phokas, whom you seek; do what you are commanded." The astonished soldiers would not lift a hand against him. Then Phokas added: "It is not you who kill me, but those who sent you hither; therefore execute your orders." After a long parley, the soldiers, who were accustomed to obey orders, consented to behead him. St. Phokas is represented as a gardener with a sword in his hand.

MARTYRDOM OF THE THEBAN LEGION.

DURING the time of Diocletian and Maximian, there was in Egypt a Roman legion of Christian soldiers. On account of a rebellion in Gaul the legion was called to Rome. From Rome it was sent to the encampment on the Rhone. The Emperor Maximian wished to offer sacrifice to the gods in presence of the Gallic commander and the entire army. The Christian legion refused to participate in this ceremony. The emperor, enraged at the refusal, ordered every tenth man to be beheaded. Still the survivors refused to accede to the emperor's demands. For the second time he ordered every tenth man to be beheaded. After a third refusal, he ordered the entire legion to be executed. The heathen soldiers carried out the order, and the blood of these martyrs flowed from the encampment into the river. After the entire legion had suffered a glorious martyrdom, Mauritius, the colonel, was slain.

DEATH OF FORTY HOLY MARTYRS.

THE Roman emperor Licinius ordered, in the year 320, that each of his subjects, under pain of death, should offer sacrifice to the gods. His governor, Agricola, accordingly, ordered the soldiers of the Twelfth Legion to be summoned from St. Sebastian. Thereupon forty warriors stepped forth from the ranks and fearlessly acknowleged their Christian faith. The governor at first sought, through flatteries and promises, to persuade them to sacrifice to the gods. Not being able to accomplish his purpose, he had them scourged, and after having them torn with iron nails, had them cast into prison. After a few days the commander-in-chief, Lysias, sought to conquer the firmness of the confessors. But he was vanquished. Thereupon the governor had the forty soldiers summoned before him on a day which would freeze the blood, and, divested of all clothing, had them placed on a table covered with frost and ice. Near by, a bath of lukewarm water was placed, in order to induce the frozen confessors to yield. One of them, overcome by terrible cold, was lifted from off the table and placed in the bath. Scarce was he in the water when he expired. Seeing this, a soldier in attendance, inspired by the grace of God, divested himself of his clothing, and took his place with the now half-dead martyrs. After the glorious heroes had ceased to exist, the governor ordered their bodies to be burned on a funeral pyre. The forty martyrs are represented standing on an ice-covered table, with palm branches in their hands.

THE MIRACLE OF ST. BLASIUS.

WHEN Bishop Blasius was in prison, a boy was brought to him who had a fishbone in his throat. No doctor could extract it. The anxious mother led her son to the feet of the saint and implored his help. The saint prayed, laid hands on the sufferer, and made the sign of the cross over him. The boy was immediately relieved. After the death of the saint, many persons were relieved of throat diseases through his intercession. The Church, accordingly, blesses the throats of the people on the feast of St. Blasius.

DEATH OF ST. BLASIUS.

ST. BLASIUS was Bishop of Sebaste, in Armenia. During the persecution of the Christians under the rule of the Emperor Licinius he fled to a neighboring town and hid in a cavern. The officials who were in pursuit of him found him and led him back to Sebaste. Judge Agricola sought, through flattery and promises, and then through tortures, such as brutal laceration of his flesh with sharp iron instruments, to make him renounce the faith. Finally, after the saint had proved to be immovable despite of promises and tortures, he was beheaded.

THE SPIDER'S WEB A DEFENSIVE WALL.

During the time of the persecution of the Christians, St. Felix was a priest at Nola. By command of the emperor, soldiers were sent to capture and kill him. Felix escaped through a gap of a ruined wall. The soldiers discovered this, and pursued him. But in the meantime a spider had spread its web across the hole. The soldiers concluded from this that no man could have gone in there, and accordingly hastened on. Hence, St. Felix escaped death by means of a spider's web. St. Paulinus makes this remark concerning the circumstances: "Where God is, a spider's web becomes the strongest wall; where God is not, the strongest wall is but a spider's web. Who shall not rejoice, therefore, to serve a God who guards His children in such a powerful and loving manner?"

ST. NICHOLAS.

WHEN the holy Bishop Nicholas was as yet a simple priest, it chanced that a noble family, formerly very distinguished and opulent, through ill-fortune was reduced to a state of indigence. He thought he could not devote his money to a better purpose than that of saving this family from utter ruin. When he considered, however, how hard it is for those who have fallen from wealth to accept alms, he threw a sum of money, during the night, through the window, into the sleeping-room of the head of the family. This enabled the man to sustain his family and to have his eldest daughter married. Some time afterward the saint did the same act, for the second and third time, so that the father was enabled to attend to the needs of his two other daughters. But the third time, the saint flinging the money into the sleeping-chamber, the father suddenly woke up. He at once rushed out in pursuit of his benefactor, and, on overtaking him, flung himself at his feet, expressing his profoundest gratitude. The saint begged the man never to mention the incident to any one. But the latter told everybody of his acquaintance of the noble deed. The church celebrates the feast of St. Nicholas on the 6th of December. In some countries good children even yet receive presents on that day.

ST. MARTIN AND THE BEGGAR.

St. Martin served as a Christian soldier in the Roman army. While, one cold day in winter, he was riding through the streets of Amiens, he was asked for alms by a half-naked beggar. Martin cut his cloak in two, and handed one half to the shivering beggar. The next night, Christ appeared to him wearing the half of the cloak that Martin had given to the beggar, and said to the angels that surrounded Him: "Martin presented Me with this garment." The house in which this vision occurred was afterward turned into a church. St. Martin has since been painted as a Roman cavalier handing half of his cloak to a beggar.

ST. MARTIN'S DISCHARGE FROM THE ROMAN ARMY.

St. Martin in order to devote himself to a religious life, requested his discharge from his commanding officer. The latter, enraged at this request, accused Martin of wishing to withdraw from the army through a motive of cowardice, as a battle with the Germans was impending. Martin answered: "I will prove to you that faith, not cowardice, induces me to resign from the army. I will place myself, without arms, in the front rank of the army, and with no other weapon than the sign of the cross will meet the enemy." The commander had him thrown into prison, in order to have him on the day of battle exposed to the swords of the enemy. But God so ordained that, instead of precipitating battle, the Germans sued for peace. Then Martin received his discharge without further trouble.

MIRACLE BY ST. MARTIN.

When St. Martin was consecrated Bishop of Tours he endeavored to destroy the worship of idols existing in some portions of his bishopric. He found near a certain heathen temple a gigantic fir-tree. The heathens said to him: "We will cut down this tree, and if you catch it in your arms, you will prove to us the power of your God." Martin immediately advanced, and allowed his feet to be tied, so that he could not escape. When the tree fell, Martin made the sign of the cross, and caught it in his arms without suffering the least injury.

On another occasion, Martin entered a pagan village. The inhabitants hastened to see the miracle-worker. While he was proclaiming to them the truths of the Gospel, a woman brought the dead body of her son, and besought the saint, in the most tearful manner, to restore him to life. Moved by the tears of the mother, and by the thought of winning the pagans to the Christian faith through a miracle, the saint threw himself on his knees and prayed. Immediately the dead boy arose to life. In this manner St. Martin succeeded in extirpating paganism and the worship of idols in his bishopric, and even beyond it.

CONSTANTINE, THE FIRST CHRISTIAN EMPEROR.

In the year 306, the Emperors Constantine and Maxentius were facing one another in Italy, ready for battle. The sword was to decide which of the two would be emperor of the entire Roman Empire. Constantine had no real trust in the gods, and before the battle invoked the aid of the God of the Christians. Thereupon, at noonday, in the sight of the whole army, a Cross appeared in the heavens, with the inscription : "In this sign thou shalt conquer." Full of hope, Constantine had a banner made bearing the figure of the Cross, and led his army to battle. He defeated his opponent Maxentius, and was then Emperor of the whole Roman Empire. Thankful for the assistance received, he immediately put a stop to the persecution of the Christians, and granted them protection and freedom of worship. During his entire reign he remained well disposed towards the Christians. When Constantine's end drew near, he was baptized. He was the first Christian emperor, and died in 337.

HOW BISHOP SPIRIDION CONVERTED THE ARIANS.

AT the famous Œcumenical Council of Nice, held in 325, there were present 318 bishops, assembled from all parts of the world. A most learned man defended before the council the false doctrines of Arius, who denied the divinity of Christ, with marvelous adroitness. Even the most able bishops tried in vain to convince this opponent of the error of his assertions.

Then Bishop Spiridion arose to speak. The other bishops were apprehensive that he could not argue against so learned a man, on account of his lack of knowledge. But Spiridion simply gave an exposition of the living faith, as believed and taught by the Catholic Church concerning the divinity of Christ.

After Spiridion had ceased speaking, the learned man remained silent for a while; then he said: "I am now convinced of the truth of the Catholic Church. I have contended so long, as it was only a war of words; but now that the divine truth has been placed before me in all its true simplicity, I admit myself conquered. And I earnestly advise you all to submit to the true doctrine as explained by this man."

A JUDGMENT OF GOD.

ARIUS was a heretic, who, in the time of Constantine, denied the divinity of Christ. Several bishops of the Roman Church followed him in his false teachings, and hence his heresies spread with rapidity. At the celebrated Council of Nice, in 325, these doctrines were considered and condemned. Arius and his followers won over the emperor to their aid, through flattery, and the latter commanded the Bishop of Constantinople to adopt the doctrines of Arius. As Arius and his followers were marching through Constantinople in triumph, he was stricken by the hand of God. He stepped aside to answer a call of nature, but did not return. He was found dead shortly afterward, with his bowels voided.

A BISHOP BEFORE A JUDGE.

The Greek emperor Valens espoused the Arian heresy. In order to make his entire empire Arian, he traveled over its different provinces. Bishop Basilius of Cæsarea was then the most zealous and able defender of Catholic doctrine. The emperor, regarding him as the greatest obstacle in his way, decided to have him removed. Basilius was brought before the judge. To the threats of the judge, Basilius answered: "A man who has nothing, does not fear that his goods may be taken from him. Banishment has no dread for me, as I regard the whole earth as the possession of God. Neither am I afraid of death, as it will only bring me the nearer to God, for whom I live and for whom I yearn." The judge replied: "Never before has a man spoken to me with such frankness." Basilius bravely answered: "That comes from the fact that you never had any relations with bishops; for, if you had, you would receive a similar answer under the same circumstances." When the judge told the Emperor Valens that this man could not be moved, he determined to send him into banishment. But as he was signing the order, he broke three pens, one after another. He then renounced his purpose, and left the bishop in his diocese.

THE EMPEROR LEO THE ICONOCLAST AND THE PATRIARCH NICEPHORUS.

THE Greek emperor Leo III. was a violent hater of Christian images. Both by cunning and violence he sought to abolish the pious practice of showing them reverence. He concluded, however, that he could not accomplish his purpose unless he could win over to his side Nicephorus, the Patriarch of Constantinople. Leo thereupon strove to convince the Patriarch that the true faith forbade paying honor to images, and said: "Did not Moses forbid the making of the likeness of men, or of any other thing?" The Patriarch answered: "Moses forbade his people to make any images to be worshiped, as the Jews had seen them worshiped in Egypt. It is one thing to worship an image, and another to have simply brought to our minds the person whom that image represents."

Leo would not be convinced by this explanation, but sent the Patriarch into exile. All the clergy who would not destroy the images in their churches he cast into prison or put to death. He placed in the banished Patriarch's seat a bad man who was willing to obey him in all things. Accordingly, all the walls of the churches whereon were painted the acts and sufferings of Christ and the saints were whitewashed over. Sculptured or carved images were thrown down, broken or burnt.

ST. PATRICK, APOSTLE OF IRELAND.—HOW ST. ODRAN SAVED THE SAINT'S LIFE.

ST. PATRICK, the Apostle of Ireland, was taken captive in his youth by King Niall, in one of his raids into Gaul. He served seven years in bondage as a swineherd, with Milcho, a chief who lived in the County Antrim. Having escaped to Gaul, he had a vision in which he heard the voice of the Irish crying out: "We entreat thee, holy youth, to come and walk still among us." Patrick was deeply affected by this vision, and he was subsequently commissioned, to his great joy, by Pope Celestine, to bear the faith of Christ to the pagan Irish. His mission was miraculously successful. He won the entire nation to the doctrines of Christ without a drop of blood having been shed through persecution, a fact unexampled in the history of Christianity.

But there was one martyr during his mission. A certain idolater named Failge, a great adversary of Christ, resolved to kill the saint, who had destroyed the idols to which he was bound. Odran, Patrick's driver or charioteer, having discovered the danger, requested his master to change places with him in the chariot, pretending that he was greatly fatigued. The saint, always happy to exercise his humility, gladly acquiesced. Ere long they arrived at the spot where the assassin lay in ambush, and as they were passing, the wretch rushed forward, and mistaking the driver for the servant, pierced Odran with a spear. The saint now understood Odran's motive, and his grief was great over his pious and devoted disciple. The vengeance of God fell on the murderer, for he died on the same day. St. Odran is "the only Irish martyr on record that suffered in Ireland by the hands of an Irishman."

DEATH OF ST. PATRICK.

DURING his missionary life St. Patrick visited every part of Ireland, consecrating bishops, ordaining priests, and fostering the religion of Christ everywhere. Toward the close of his life, having the happiness of seeing the entire nation within the Christian fold, he confined his labors almost exclusively to his own Archdiocese of Armagh. Previous to his death he was forewarned that he should not die in Armagh, but in Saul, "a favorite retreat which he had built upon the land given him by his first convert, Dicho." Having repaired to the monastery of Saul, he awaited joyously the hour of his entrance into eternal bliss. Being admonished by his guardian angel as to the time of his death, says the chronicler, he fortified himself with the *divine mysteries*, from the hand of his disciple, the holy bishop Tassach, and lifting up his eyes, he beheld the heavens opened, and Jesus standing in the midst of a multitude of angels. Then raising his hands and blessing his people, and giving thanks, he passed out of this world, from the faith unto the reality, from his pilgrimage unto his country, from transitory pain unto eternal glory.

A MIRACLE BY THE HOLY ABBOT ROMAN.

THE holy abbot Roman was once traveling, with a pious brother monk, to visit the grave of the holy martyr Mauritius. They were overtaken by night on the way, and they took refuge in a mountain cave. Two lepers lived in the cave. Meantime they were out gathering wood. On their return they were astonished to find two men in their cave, and they at once made known their horrible disease. Roman did not flee, however, but embraced and kissed both, and remained with them over night. Next morning, accompanied by the brother, he resumed his journey. They had not gone far before they were overtaken by the two lepers. The latter threw themselves at the feet of Roman and thanked him with tearful delight, for both had been completely healed of their horrible disease.

THE LEGEND OF ST. CHRISTOPHORUS.

St. Christophorus's original name was Reprobus. He was a pagan, and of gigantic strength. He was proud of his great powers, and he resolved never to serve any one save the most powerful person on earth. He traveled over mountain and valley in many lands. At length he came to a king who was represented to him as being the most powerful man living. He entered the king's service, and the latter was proud of his giant. Once a man sang before the king an old song describing the power of Satan. Thereupon the king marked himself with the sign of the cross. The giant arose and asked the king why he crossed himself. The king answered: "When I make this sign, the power of Satan cannot hurt me." "Then," answered Reprobus, "I can no longer serve you, but will go in search of him who is more powerful than you."

He went into the wilderness, in search of Satan, and boldly marched forward to him, when he appeared, and offered him his service. The bargain was soon made, and Reprobus was Satan's servant. They traveled on over field and desert. At last they came to a spot where a plain cross was erected bearing an image of the crucified Saviour. On seeing this, Satan would not dare advance another step, but, turning hastily around, walked back. When Reprobus saw this, he asked him: "Why do you fly before that sign?" Satan answered: "I must fly from that sign, for it represents Christ, who conquered me on the cross." On hearing this, Reprobus left Satan, and traveled on till he met a hermit. The latter said to him: "Jesus Christ is the most powerful Being of all; whosoever will serve Him must watch, fast and pray." Reprobus answered, "I cannot do that; I will serve Him in some other manner." Then the hermit led him on to a river and said: "Build yourself a hut here, and carry the travelers over this stream for the love of the Lord." Reprobus worked untiringly night and day to carry out the command of the hermit. One night he heard a child calling. He immediately arose, lifted it tenderly on his shoulders, and, supported by his stout staff, carried it through the waves. In the middle of the river, the child grew heavier, and at last Reprobus cried out anxiously: "O child, how heavy you are!" The child answered: "You are, in truth, carrying not only the whole world, but Him that created the heavens and the earth." He baptized the giant in the water, and said: "I am Jesus Christ, and I baptize thee, that thou mayest henceforth be a Christian, and bear the name of Christophorus." And Christophorus remained a steadfast Christian. At last, when a pagan king sought to compel him to offer sacrifice to the false gods, he laid his head under the ax, and died for Christ, his Lord.

PATIENCE OF ST. EPHRAIM.

ST. EPHRAIM, after a long and weakening fast, said to a brother of the order, who was accustomed to serve him: "Dear brother, bring me something to eat, for I am very weak." The brother hastened to obey the command of the reverend father. He hastily prepared a meal and was bringing it to the father's cell, when, unluckily, he stumbled and let the plate drop, spilling the contents and breaking the plate into pieces. Overcome with shame, the good brother could only blush and look at the results of his negligence on the floor, in the form of broken pieces and scattered food. St. Ephraim saw the accident and smilingly remarked, in his softest tones: "Be not disturbed, dear brother; since our meal has not come to us, we will go to the meal." And so saying, he sat down on the floor patiently and partook of the scattered fragments of the frugal repast.

ST. MONICA'S MATERNAL LOVE.

ST. MONICA, mother of St. Augustine, the illustrious Bishop of Hippo, was born in Numidia, now Algeria, Africa, in the year 332. Her husband was a pagan, and a man of violent temper and many vices. The ambition of Augustine's father was to give his son a finished education, so that he would rise in the world. Monica seconded her husband in his desire, but her hope was that her son would devote his cultured talents to the glory of God.

In his seventeenth year Augustine went to Carthage to study rhetoric. While there he fell into bad company, contracted evil habits, and espoused the Manichæan heresy. Monica, on learning this, was inconsolable. She forbade her son to eat at her table or sleep beneath her roof thereafter. This severity she exercised to cause him to reflect on his errors. Her days and nights were passed in tears and prayers for the conversion of the son, so much so that a good bishop once consoled her with the remark: "It is impossible that a child of such tears should perish." She followed her son in all his travels from city to city, redoubling her prayers and her tears. When he set out for Rome to teach rhetoric, Monica, fearing the associations of the great pagan city might delay his conversion, followed him and found him at Milan, where the great St. Ambrose was then archbishop. Here she renewed her prayers and exhortations, and finally had the consolation of seeing her illustrious son baptized by the hands of St. Ambrose. Monica then was ready to die; she had no more to live for; her prayers had been heard; her happiness was complete. On her way home with her now converted son she was seized with a fever and died in Italy, where she was buried. St. Monica has ever been regarded as the model of mothers, and many churches throughout the world have been erected in her honor.

ST. AUGUSTINE.

St. Augustine, busied in thought, was walking one day along the seashore. He was pondering on the mystery of the Blessed Trinity, and thinking how he could solve it. Suddenly he saw a little boy dipping water from the seashore into a hole he had dug in the sand. The saint asked the little boy: "What are you doing here?" The boy answered: "I am going to empty the sea into this little hole." The saint smiled and said: "That is impossible." "Well," replied the boy, "I will have the sea emptied into this little hole sooner than you will have solved the mystery of the Blessed Trinity." Then the boy vanished.

KING THEODOSIUS AND ARCHBISHOP AMBROSE.

WHEN St. Ambrose was Archbishop of Milan, the Roman emperor Theodosius resided there. This emperor had, on account of a revolt in Thessalonica in which several imperial officials had been stoned, ordered seven thousand men to be surrounded in the amphitheatre by soldiers and slaughtered on the spot. When this terrible news reached Milan, St. Ambrose wrote a letter to the emperor wherein he commanded him to make public penance for so grievous a crime. But when Theodosius arrived at the vestibule of the church, Ambrose met him. He upbraided him for the crime of having shed so much innocent blood, and forbade him to enter the church. The emperor acknowledged his crime, and stood by the door of the church in open penitence, while he implored

God, on his knees, in tearful supplication, to grant him pardon. The people were so moved on seeing this exhibition of public penance, that they wept with the repentant emperor. But Ambrose was not satisfied with that, for he exacted from the emperor a promise that, during his future life, he would never allow the death-sentence to be executed until thirty days after the death-warrant had been signed by him, so as to give him time for reconsideration. Theodosius promulgated this law, and Ambrose received him once more into the communion of the faithful.

THE POWER OF THE SIGN OF THE CROSS.

ONCE the monks of a certain monastery whose abbot had just died came to St. Benedict and implored him to become the head of their institution. He accepted, but the monks found themselves deceived in him. He was too rigorous for their ideas, and he would not tolerate their disobedience of the rules. The virulence against him at length went so far that some of them resolved to kill him. They put poison in the wine which was placed on the table before the holy man when taking his frugal meal. Benedict, as was his wont, made the sign of the cross over the victuals he was about to eat, and immediately the glass that contained the wine burst into fragments. The holy man recognized from this that a death-dose had been placed before him, from the effects of which he had been saved by the sign of life. He immediately arose and said to the assembled monks: "Brothers, may the Almighty God have mercy on you! Why did you do such a thing in regard to me? Did I not always tell you that your morals and mine did not harmonize? Go now and find a superior who will suit your morals better. From this moment you will not have me at your head any more." And so saying, he left the monastery and returned once more to his beloved desert solitude.

HOW ST. BENEDICT RESCUED HIS BELOVED PUPIL MAURUS FROM DROWNING.

St. Benedict had two pupils, named Maurus and Placidus. One day he sent Placidus to a pond near by to bring some water. Placidus hastened to obey the command of the beloved father. But while engaged in drawing the water he fell into the pond. St. Benedict saw in spirit Placidus struggling with death, and sent Maurus at once to his aid. Maurus asked his blessing, hastened to the pond, and rescued Placidus. When they had come ashore, Maurus recollected that he had walked on the surface of the water, and he ascribed the miracle to the blessing of his beloved father. Benedict, however, assured him it was God who had performed the miracle, as a reward for his prompt obedience.

ST. BENEDICT AND TOTILA.

St. Benedict was endowed with the gifts of working miracles and of prophecy. Totila, King of the Goths, wished to put him to the test. He informed the saint that he was to pay him a visit, but sent instead one of his servants named Rippo, in kingly attire, attended by a gorgeous retinue. Benedict saw them coming and called to Rippo from a distance, "My son, put by what you have on—they do not belong to you." Rippo and his attendants were surprised, and told the king how the royal robes did not deceive Benedict. Totila then personally visited the holy man and prostrated himself reverently at his feet. Benedict said : " You do much that is wrong, and you have done much that is wicked. Renounce your evil ways. You will reign nine years, and you shall die in the tenth." Totila was deeply troubled at these words, implored the holy man to pray for him, and renounced his cruel ways. The saint's prophecy was fulfilled.

LEO THE GREAT IN PRESENCE OF GENSERIC.

Scarce had Italy torn herself from the grip of the Huns, when Genseric, King of the Vandals, landed on her shores with a great fleet, in the year 455. Carrying fire and sword everywhere he went, he at length approached Rome. Pope Leo went forward to meet him, as three years before he had met the terrible Attila. He did not succeed in having the city wholly spared this time, however. Genseric stormed

Rome, but did not destroy it. He did not murder as he went; he simply plundered the city, and then returned to Africa.

THE HUNS BEFORE PARIS, AND ST. GENEVIEVE.

In the fifth century, King Attila, with his Huns, bore down on Europe from the East. He destroyed all before him. Nobody could withstand him. At length he marched for the great city of Paris. When the inhabitants heard of his approach they were sorely troubled. They resolved to fly from the city with all their portable goods. At this time St. Genevieve lived in the city. She came out of her cloister and calling the women of Paris together, she implored them to pray fervently. She also addressed the men, telling them to remove none of their goods, as, through the interposition of God, they would be spared. And so it happened. St. Genenevieve obtained from God, through her prayers and the prayers of the people of Paris, the request she asked. The Huns passed by the city without attacking it. From that time to the present day St. Genevieve is honored as the patron saint of Paris.

ST. PAULINUS AS A SLAVE.

AT the time when the Vandals were ravaging Italy with fire and sword and carrying off the inhabitants into slavery, St. Paulinus was Bishop of Nola. One day a widow came to him filled with grief, and told him that the barbarians had carried off her son. The holy bishop could give her no advice, as he had no money wherewith to ransom the captive. In this difficulty he resolved to give himself up as a slave in the place of the widow's son. He went to Africa, accompanied by the mother. The son was soon found. His master willingly took the bishop, whose dignity he knew not, in place of the widow's son, as a slave. For a long time the bishop worked as a gardener. When, at length, his master discovered his true character, and that he had, of his own free will, become a slave, he generously gave him his freedom. He even asked him to demand any favor he wished. Paulinus asked nothing but the freedom of all the prisoners from Nola. Honored by the Vandals, who were astonished at his magnanimous action, Paulinus returned to Nola with the released slaves, where he was received by the people amid general rejoicings. In remembrance of this noble action, the saint is represented in bishop's vestments, with a broken chain in his hand.

ST. ARBOGAST RESTORES A KING'S SON TO LIFE.

The only son of King Dagobert went one day to the chase. While his companions had scattered through the forest with the hounds, a wild boar rushed forth. His horse took fright and threw him from the saddle. He hung from the stirrups and was dragged along by the frightened animal. After a long search he was found by the hunters, and amid loud lamentations was borne to his home. He died the next day. The sorrow of the people mingled with that of his parents. Following the advice of his people, the king sent a messenger to St. Arbogast, Bishop of Strasburg. The latter immediately set forth. The king and the bishop could scarce exchange words on account of their grief. The queen came forward and fell on her knees, weeping aloud. The bishop, sympathizing with her in her anguish, lifted her to her feet. Without waiting for any refreshment after his journey, Arbogast retired to the church. Before the shades of evening fell, he entered the room where the dead young man lay. God did not leave his servant long in anxious suspense. While Arbogast was praying the young man raised his head. Overcome with joy, the saint raised the boy to his feet. Then he ordered that the shroud should be removed, and the prince clothed in his royal attire.

Those who were present could not restrain themselves from breaking out in cries of joy. The king and queen were lifted from the depths of sorrow to the pinnacle of joy. They offered the richest gifts to the saint. The latter, however, would accept nothing, but simply expressed his desire that in thanksgiving to God the king should make an offering to the Church of Our Blessed Lady in Strasburg. St. Arbogast is honored as the patron saint of Strasburg to the present day.

ST. ISIDORE, A PEASANT.

St. Isidore was a peasant in Spain. He worked for a nobleman. He was as zealous in the service of God as he was in the service of his employer. He attended Mass every day before beginning work. Some evil-disposed persons told his employer that he had neglected his work. The nobleman went out to the field early one morning to see if Isidore was at work. He was surprised to see the youth, clad in white, following the plow at such an early hour. From that moment the nobleman placed the fullest confidence in his servant, and allowed him to attend his devotions without remonstrance. The Church celebrates the feast of St. Isidore on the 10th of May.

HONESTY OF ST. ELIGIUS.

THE holy Bishop Eligius was in early youth apprenticed to an honest goldsmith. Subsequently King Chlotar II. had his attention drawn to the skill of young Eligius. He asked him to build a royal throne, and gave him a large amount of gold and precious stones for the purpose. After a time, Eligius brought the throne to the king. The king was lost in admiration of the exquisite workmanship displayed, and ordered that a rich reward should be granted to Eligius. Thereupon Eligius produced a royal footstool, and said that there was enough gold remaining to make another. The king was deeply moved at the young man's honesty. He insisted that Eligius should reside in his palace, and made him a master of the mint. Eligius objected to the taking of the customary oath of fidelity. When pressed by the king, he burst into tears. He did not wish to offend the king, and at the same time he would not perform an act to which he had conscientious objections. The king then withdrew his command, consoled Eligius, and said: "It is well. Your objection to swear gives me more confidence in you than if you had taken a hundred oaths."

HOW ST. CUTHBERT RULED WIND AND FIRE.

MORE than a thousand years ago, St. Cuthbert was superior of a monastery in England. But not alone in the monastery did he serve God with a holy zeal, but he traveled throughout the most distant districts, instructing the ignorant in the word of God. In one of his missions he entered the house of a woman whom he had long known. A fire broke out in the village. A violent wind blew the fiery sparks from roof to roof. The anxious woman implored the holy Cuthbert that her house and the village might not be destroyed. The saint replied: "Do not be troubled, the fire will not injure you." He then went to the door and prayed. Immediately the wind changed and turned the flames toward the other side, where there were no houses, and the village was saved.

HOW GOD PROVIDED ST. CUTHBERT AND HIS PUPIL WITH FOOD.

St. Cuthbert, accompanied by a boy, was once traveling on a mission. Both were tired and hungry, and as yet at a long distance from their destination. The boy complained that they had nothing with them, and that nothing could be procured. The saint replied: "You must have faith and hope in God, for no one wants who serves Him faithfully." While they were thus talking, the road led them along the bank of a stream, where they saw an eagle perched on a rock. St. Cuthbert said to the boy: "Hurry thither and bring us what the Lord sends us through this messenger." The boy returned with a large fish, which the eagle had just caught. St. Cuthbert then remarked: "But, my son, why did you not give a share to the messenger? Quick, go and bring him half, as a reward for his services." The boy did so. The other half they prepared when they came to the nearest house, and satisfied the appetites of both themselves and the family.

HOW THE HERMIT AGATHO TAUGHT HIS PUPILS CONSCIENTIOUSNESS.

THE aged father Agatho lived the life of a hermit for many years in the wilderness. One day he was traveling with his scholars, when one of them found a package of peas on the road. He said to Agatho: "Father, if you order me to do so, I shall bring it along." The aged man looked at him in astonishment and replied: "Did you leave that bundle here?" "No." Agatho answered: "Why, then, should you take with you something which you did not leave here?"

THE CHARITABLE ABBOT ODILO.

As St. Martin divided his cloak with a beggar, so the Abbot Odilo gave his garment to the dead. He was traveling, on a certain occasion, through a portion of the country afflicted by famine. On the way, he found two naked children who had died of hunger and cold. He got down from his horse, wrapped the bodies in his overcoat, and paid some persons living near by to help him to bury them. He then continued on his journey. As the famine lasted several years, the charitable Odilo sold his sacred altar-vessels and ornaments and a golden crown that King Henry of Germany had presented to his monastery, and supported the poor with the proceeds.

HOW THE ANGLO-SAXONS RECEIVED CHRISTIANITY.

SOME young Anglo-Saxons were once standing in the Roman market to be sold as slaves. Gregory the Great happened to pass near them, and he stopped to admire their handsome figures and noble bearing. He asked to what nation they belonged. He was told they were Angles. "Well," he replied, "be angels, and the kingdom of heaven shall be yours." When he afterward became Pope he sent missionaries to England to convert the people to Christianity. The Angles received the faith readily, and became zealous Christians.

They sent St. Boniface and many other holy missionaries to convert the Germans.

DEATH OF ST. KILIAN AND HIS COMPANIONS.

ST. KILIAN, accompanied by two companions, went from Ireland to the vicinity of Wurzburg to preach the Gospel. The fame of his deeds reached the ears of Duke Gosbert. The latter had Kilian summoned to his court, listened to him with attention, immediately renounced his idolatry, and with several of his courtiers received holy baptism. But St. Kilian's joy over his success was marred by the knowledge that Gosbert had married Gailana, the wife of his living brother. Gosbert promised the saint to dismiss his wife, and then proceeded on a campaign. Gailana, however, heard of what was in contemplation. She wickedly took the terrible resolve to have the holy bishop and his companions murdered. She gave for this purpose a large sum of money to two of her servants. These forced their way at early morning into the sleeping-chambers of the castle, and drawing their swords, slew the bishop and those who accompanied him.

ST. TRUDBERT IN THE BLACK FOREST.

MORE than a thousand years ago, St. Trudbert went from Rome as a pilgrim and took up his abode in the Munster Valley, in the upper Black Forest. Count Ottbert, to whom the country belonged, gave him a tract of uncultivated land whereon to build a monastery. He also gave him the assistance of six men to clear the ground and erect the building. After St. Trudbert had lived there four years as a hermit, and had given advice and aid to all those who visited him, he was slain by two wicked men. His body was buried in the chapel. On this spot a large Benedictine monastery was afterward erected, from which were sent many zealous missionaries to win over the heathens of the surrounding country to the Church of Christ. In the beginning of this century this monastery was still standing. The last of its abbots ordered, in bitter grief, that a gravestone should be erected to him with a representation of soldiers casting dice, accompanied with the inscription: "My clothes they have divided among them, and for my garment they have cast lots." His request was fulfilled, and the stone stands near the spot where the saint to whom the monastery owed its origin and name, twelve hundred years previously, met his death.

ST. OTTILIA AND THE LEPER.

ST. OTTILIA was a daughter of a duke in Alsace. As she had a great desire to enter the cloister, she received from her father the Castle of Hohenburg, which she converted into a convent for women. Gradually a large number of young women joined her, and, under her guidance, lived a holy life. She also built a hospital and tended the sick. On one occasion a man who was afflicted with leprosy appeared at the door, emitting an unbearable odor. The abbess wished to bring him something to eat. The aspect of the leper was so horrible, however, that she felt like withdrawing from his presence. But Ottilia suddenly resolved to conquer this natural weakness. She took the wretched man in her arms, as if he were a feeble child, and put the food into his mouth. She wept with pity, and prayed: "Lord, restore him to health, or grant him patience." No sooner had the leper finished his meal than he was wholly cured.

ST. BRIDGET'S CHOICE.

St. Bridget, Patroness of Ireland, accompanied by her nuns, was, on a certain occasion, in the presence of Bishop Maccelle, from whom she had received the veil, and she asked the good bishop to give them a brief instruction on some pious subject. The bishop delivered a brief discourse on the "Eight Beatitudes." Whereupon the saint, turning to her sister nuns, said: "We are eight virgins, and eight virtues are offered to us as a means of sanctification. It is true that whoever practices one virtue perfectly must possess every other; yet let each of us now choose a virtue for special devotion."

St. Bridget, as superioress, was requested to make the first choice, and she chose that sweetest of all virtues, *Mercy*. Her whole life afterward was a living illustration of the virtue which she had chosen.

ST. BONIFACE AND THE ANCIENT OAK.

ST. BONIFACE preached the gospel to the Hessians. They reverenced a very ancient oak, and offered sacrifice under it to their thunder-god, Thor. The saint looked on this pagan practice with detestation, and proceeded to cut down the tree. The pagans standing around believed that Thor would avenge this outrage by striking Boniface dead with lightning at the first stroke of the ax. But the tree fell, and the saint stood unhurt. On seeing this, the pagan Hessians renounced their false gods and embraced Christianity. Out of the wood of this oak St. Boniface built a chapel, which he dedicated to St. Peter.

MARTYRDOM OF ST. BONIFACE.

When St. Boniface was an old man of eighty-five years, his zeal for the welfare of souls kept him as busy as when in the heyday of his vigor. He delivered over the Archbishopric of Mayence to his pupil Lullus, and with several companions set out to convert the pagan Frisians. He instructed and baptized many thousands of them. At length came the 5th of June, the eve of the feast of Whitsuntide, when he was to administer the holy sacrament of confirmation to the new converts. Boniface had tents erected in the open field, and, engaged in prayer, awaited the arrival of those about to be confirmed. Suddenly, however, a mob of armed pagan Frisians burst in upon him. His attendants and the new converts wished to defend him, but Boniface came forward and said: "Children, do not fight. This is the day for which I have this many a year longed. The hour of my freedom has now come. Be constant, brothers, and fear nothing which cannot harm your souls. Calmly complete the short road to death which will lead you into the heavenly kingdom." Then holding the gospel over his head, he received his death-blow. With St. Boniface fifty-two companions suffered martyrdom. His remains are buried in Fulda.

CHARLEMAGNE AND BISHOP LUDGERUS.

CHARLEMAGNE once summoned the holy Ludgerus, Bishop of Munster, to his palace. The saint went. But when the messenger arrived to lead him into the presence of the emperor, he found the bishop reading his breviary. He replied that he would comply with the command as soon as he had finished his prayers. Some of his enemies sought to arouse the emperor's anger on account of this delay. When Ludgerus appeared before his majesty, the emperor indignantly asked why he had compelled him to wait. The bishop mildly answered: "I know my obligations to your majesty. But I believed you would not be indignant if I gave God the preference. Your imperial majesty, in appointing me bishop, commanded me to serve God in preference to men."

This answer made such an impression on the mind of the emperor that he treated him with the greatest consideration, while the bishop's enemies fell into disgrace.

THE PATRIARCH IGNATIUS AND THE SCHISMATIC PHOTIUS.

THE Greek emperor Michael III. entertained a violent hatred for the Patriarch Ignatius of Constantinople, banished him, and placed a sycophant named Photius in the patriarchal chair. Photius wrote a hypocritical and mendacious letter to the Pope, saying that Ignatius had resigned, that he himself had been forced to accept the patriarchal dignity, and that he, therefore, prayed for his holiness's recognition. The Pope detected the trick, and excommunicated Photius. The latter, however, through the favor of the new emperor, Basil, retained the patriarchal seat eleven years, and gathered around him all those bishops opposed to the Pope. But when the emperor saw the great discontent that such a state of affairs produced among his subjects, he dared no longer protect so dangerous a man, and he recalled the Patriarch Ignatius from exile. The latter at once set to work to heal the wounds inflicted on the Church. When, worn out by suffering and old age, he died, in 878, Photius again resumed the patriarchal seat, and continued his evil conduct. The schism which he caused continues to the present day in the Eastern Church.

MIRACLE BY THE HOLY BISHOP ULRICH.

BISHOP ULRICH OF AUGSBURG on a certain occasion received a visit from his friend, the pious Bishop Conrad of Constance. Both prelates took their meal in a house near the church. They chatted with one another on pious subjects until after midnight, when it was Friday morning. Just at that moment a messenger from the Duke of Bavaria entered the room and handed Bishop Ulrich a letter. The holy man presented to the messenger a piece of meat which lay on the table, unconscious of the fact that it was then Friday. The evil-minded messenger immediately hastened to the residence of the duke, to tell him what a hypocrite Ulrich was, inasmuch as he ate meat on Friday, and even invited himself to do so. When the slanderer wished to afford a proof of his accusation, he found to his utter discomfiture that the piece of meat was changed into a fish. Hence, the holy bishop is always represented in episcopal attire, with a fish in his hand.

THE MAGNANIMOUS BISHOP WOLFGANG.

A BEGGAR once secretly sneaked into the room of Bishop Wolfgang and cut off a large piece of the bed-curtains. As he was trying to escape he was caught by a servant, who led him into the presence of the bishop, and recommended that he should receive a severe punishment. The good bishop asked the thief why he had committed such an act. The latter answered, in tremulous accents: "Because I had no clothing, as you may see." The bishop thereupon gave him a good suit of clothes, and remarked to his servant: "If he had not been half naked he certainly would not have stolen anything. But if it happen again, then he shall be punished."

DEATH OF THE HOLY BISHOP WOLFGANG.

BISHOP WOLFGANG of Regensburg was once called to Lower Austria on important business in relation to Church property. Despite his great age and bodily weakness, he concluded that he would be able to make the long journey and attend to the business in person. While sailing down the Danube, however, he was stricken with a fatal fever, which compelled him to go ashore at the next landing-place. He gave orders that he should be carried into the church and laid on the bare floor before the altar. Here, with intense fervor, he received the most holy sacrament, and exhorted all those around him to lead good lives. As the people continued to press into the church to see the dying bishop, the sexton shut the doors. The bishop immediately said : "Open the doors and do not hinder any one from coming in, for it is no shame to die. We must fulfill this law of nature, for the Creator Himself was not ashamed to die on the cross for the sins of the world. May the Lord extend His mercy to me, and to each of you who sees me die with a contrite heart and with fear of his own death, as no one is sure of his salvation." The saint then closed his eyes and entered into the sleep of the Lord, Oct. 31, 994.

BISHOP CONRAD'S REVERENCE FOR THE MOST HOLY SACRAMENT.

WHILE Bishop Conrad of Constance was celebrating Mass in the cathedral on Easter Sunday, he perceived, just after the words of consecration had been pronounced, a spider in the chalice. Although spiders were considered poisonous, the bishop did not think of the danger to nis life, but, full of faith and trust in God, drank the contents of the chalice, spider and all. After the holy man had returned to his dwelling, he sat down by a table, with his head buried in his hands. His servants were troubled, and asked him the cause of his distress, but he only tried to console them by a few friendly words. Immediately afterward, the spider, unhurt, crawled out of his mouth. Then for the first time he related to the servants what had happened in the church, and how he had been miraculously relieved of the spider. Hence, the holy Bishop Conrad is represented with a chalice, into which a spider is descending.

BISHOP CONRAD'S GIFT OF PROPHECY.

BISHOP CONRAD of Constance returned home on a certain occasion and found a young man seated in the episcopal chair. The youth, overcome with confusion, leaped up quickly, but the bishop called him back, and said: "You will not be my successor in this seat immediately after my death. It will be another person. But the time will come when God will raise you to that dignity." And so it came to pass. After the death of Conrad, Gamonald became Bishop of Constance. The latter was succeeded by St. Gebhard. He was the young man who in a frolic had seated himself in the bishop's episcopal chair many years before.

ST. HUGO AND THE CAVALIER.

Most men during sickness think of nothing else but their sufferings. This was not the case with the holy man Hugo, however. When, during his last illness, he was visited by both clergy and laity, he made an edifying remark to each, according to their station in life or their past relations with himself. A prominent cavalier knelt with the others beside his bed and asked his blessing. Thereupon Hugo gave him this stern rebuke: "You are hurrying to eternal damnation, on account of the unjust tribute that you exact from your subjects." The cavalier was astounded on hearing such a reproach from a man who was already on the verge of the grave. He replied: "This must have been revealed to you by God Himself. True, I have recently imposed a heavy tax on my district, but it is not as yet collected. Aft r this warning, I shall not collect it."

HUMILITY OF WENCESLAUS OF BOHEMIA.

THE pious Duke Wenceslaus of Bohemia was greatly esteemed by the Emperor Otho I. During a sitting of the Imperial Diet at Worms, Otho placed the duke at his side and promised to grant him anything he pleased to ask. Wenceslaus, however, requested nothing other than an arm of St. Vitus and some of the bones of St. Sigismund. Astonished at this request, the emperor said : " You shall receive the relics on my return home, and in addition the title of king, and the privilege of bearing the imperial eagle on your banner." Wenceslaus was delighted on receiving the relics, but he declined the title of king. After his return to Prague he caused a church to be erected, in which the holy relics were deposited.

ST. WENCESLAUS'S MARTYRDOM.

The pious Duke Wenceslaus of Bohemia was bitterly hated by his wicked mother, Drahomira, and his equally wicked brother, Boleslaus. Both devised a plan to murder him. A son was born to Boleslaus, and he invited his brother to the feast given on the occasion. The saint suspected danger, but out of consideration for his brother accepted the invitation. The feast lasted till late in the night. Wenceslaus took no pleasure in the general rejoicing, and retired meantime to a church near by to pray. Drahomira saw him leave, and intimated to Boleslaus to go and accomplish their bloody purpose. Boleslaus, accompanied by several servants, surprised his brother in the church and pierced him through with a lance. Shortly afterward, many striking miracles took place at the saint's grave. The body was therefore exhumed and transferred to St. Vitus's Church, in Prague.

CANONIZATION OF THE EMPRESS CUNIGUNDE.

CUNIGUNDE was the pious and virtuous consort of the German emperor Henry I. During her husband's reign she was the ornament of his throne, a protectress of the Church and a mother to the poor. After the death of the emperor, she entered the Convent of Kaufungen. After her death there, her body was borne, amid an immense assemblage of people, to the Church of St. Peter, in Bamberg, and laid beside that of her husband. A hundred and sixty years after her death she was canonized by Pope Innocent III. On the occasion of the solemn promulgation of this act, the Pope declared that, having found, after a careful investigation, the Empress Cunigunde was possessed of complete virtue, and it having been proven that many miracles had been wrought through her intercession, he, in accordance with the advice of several bishops, enrolled the name of the empress in the calendar of the saints.

WE SHOULD CHEERFULLY FORGIVE THOSE WHO INJURE US.

ST. GUALBERT was by birth an Italian nobleman. He met, one day, in a deep valley, the murderer of his brother, against whom he had sworn mortal vengeance. When the murderer saw the brother of the man whom he had slain, accompanied by an armed retinue, he gave himself up as lost. He leaped from his horse, flung himself on the ground, crossed his arms on his breast, and awaited his death-blow. This figure of the cross on the breast of his defenseless foe reminded Gualbert of Him who on the cross prayed for His enemies. His heart was touched. He forgave the murderer of his brother and let him pass on uninjured. After Gualbert had thus spared the life of the object of his vengeance, he entered a church on the road, to pray. While reverently gazing at a crucifix before him, he saw the head of the Saviour bow toward him. Gualbert was seized with amazement and fright. He said to himself: "If God rewards the little that I have done for Him with such a great and glorious miracle, what will be the reward He will give me in heaven, if I serve Him faithfully on earth?" He immediately renounced the world, entered a neighboring Benedictine monastery, and led a holy life.

PETER THE HERMIT PREACHING THE CRUSADES.

WHEN the Mohammedans, in 1072, held the Holy Land, they ill-treated and cruelly oppressed the Christians there. They disturbed and opposed the worship of God in the holy places and plundered the pilgrims. The cries of the oppressed became louder and louder in the ears of the people of Europe. In the year 1094, Peter the Hermit, of Amiens, brought to Pope Urban III. a pressing petition from the Patriarch of Jerusalem. He described to the Holy Father in touching words the condition of the Christians of the Holy Land Tha Pope listened to the words of the holy man with heartfelt sorrow. He accordingly gave him permission to arouse the peoples of the West to undertake a crusade for the redemption of the holy places. Peter traveled through France and Italy, clad in the garb of a monk, barefooted, and riding on an ass. With crucifix in hand, he went from city to city, describing the desecration of the holy places. He was everywhere received as a messenger from heaven. His progress was one unbroken procession. Everywhere he went the people declared their determination no longer to tolerate the outrages of the Mohammedans.

ST. NORBERT AND HIS GATE-KEEPER.

THE holy Abbot Norbert was chosen Archbishop of Magdeburg. He accepted the dignity only when forced to do so by the Papal ambassador. But when he accepted his high office he did not change his rigorous mode of life. He entered Magdeburg barefooted and clad in the poorest garments. The gatekeeper of the archiepiscopal palace thought he was accosted by a beggar, and rudely ordered him away. But when the archbishop's attendant informed the gatekeeper that the apparent beggar was no other than his archbishop and master, the impudent servitor ran away in confusion. Norbert, however, called him back, and, in a pleasant voice, said to him: "Do not be alarmed, my dear brother; you have judged me far better than those who compelled me to enter this palace, of which I certainly am not worthy."

A MIRACLE BY ST. BERNARD.

The miracles performed by St. Bernard in the presence of the people were of the most remarkable character. On one occasion a woman, who was so tormented by the devil that she could no longer speak, see or hear, was brought to him in the church; she gnashed her teeth, contorted her tongue, and acted more like a monster than a human being. As often as the saint, during holy Mass, made the sign of the cross over the Sacred Host, he also made it over the woman, who had to be held down by the arms of strong men. On these occasions she would foam at the mouth and stamp with her feet. After the Pater Noster, the saint descended from the altar with the Sacred Host, held it over the woman's head, and commanded the demon, in the name of God, there present, to fly. He then ascended the steps of the altar and broke the Adorable Host. When he uttered the words, "Pax vobiscum," the demon had fled. The woman was restored, and praised God in a loud voice. The joy of the people who witnessed this miracle was boundless.

HOW FATHER FRANCIS GALUZZI CONVERTED CRIMINALS.

Father Francis Galuzzi was once called to attend a criminal under sentence of death in a prison at Rome. The unfortunate man would not listen to any advice concerning conversion or confession, and acted like a madman. Galuzzi, with tears and entreaties, prayed, like Moses: "O Lord, pardon this unhappy man, or strike me out of the book of life!" He then arose, approached the criminal and embraced him. All at once the obstinacy of the latter vanished. He confessed his sins with heartfelt contrition, and expressed himself ready to accept death as the just penalty of his crimes.

On another occasion, Father Galuzzi was called to the presence of a wealthy youth who was mortally ill. The latter had led a dissipated life, and was accustomed to utter the most horrible blasphemies. The young man received the father with repelling countenance and abruptly turned his back to him. Nevertheless, the father reminded him of the necessity of making his confession. This only aroused the anger of the youth, who burst into an access of fury and shrieked that he would never see the father again. Thus the matter stood, when the pious father asked the youth's permission to touch him with the relics of St. Francis Xavier, and to invoke the saint's intercession for him. To the great astonishment of those present, the young man did not offer the least opposition. When the prayer was ended, he made his confession with every sign of sincere contrition, pressed the crucifix to his bosom, and was converted to Christ.

THE BEASTS OF THE FOREST OBEY A SAINT.

When the Norman duke Roger was fighting the Saracens in Sicily, he came, on a certain occasion, in the neighborhood of the rock where the holy hermit Chremes dwelt. Chremes wished to testify his joy, on seeing a person who had rendered such services to Christendom, by an appropriate present. Yet, how could a poor hermit bring a present that would be worthy of a duke? But God inspired him with an idea, and gave him the means of fulfilling it. Chremes called to him those animals of the forest that are useful as human food. They gathered to him. He then led them to the duke, respectfully saluted him, and offered him the animals as a present. Roger and his companions were greatly astonished at this sight, and took great delight in it. Finally, the duke asked the hermit what means he had adopted to render the beasts so tame. Chremes replied that he had just called them from out the forest. The duke, however, did not deem it possible that a herd of wild beasts could all at once lay aside their savage instincts. Thereupon Chremes, to manifest the power of God, turned toward the animals and cried: "Since Roger will not accept you as a present, return to your forest home and enjoy your freedom." As soon as the holy man had blessed them, they rushed with joyous speed to their accustomed retreats. On seeing this, Roger descended from his horse, flung himself at the feet of Chremes, implored his blessing, and took leave of the holy man with the deepest manifestation of reverence.

ORIGIN OF CORPUS CHRISTI.

The pious Juliana lived in a convent in Luttich six hundred years ago. During prayer she had many visions. She saw the bright full moon with a piece missing. Jesus revealed to her that this break in the moon indicated the want of a feast. He charged her to institute the feast of the Most Blessed Sacrament, and to proclaim it to the world. Juliana shrunk from the task, and earnestly requested that so serious a charge be given to some distinguished and learned priest. But the Lord insisted that it should be performed by her. For twenty years the holy virgin hesitated to ask the world to inaugurate this feast. Bishop Robert of Luttich, who investigated her vision, found himself obliged to introduce this feast into his diocese. In the year 1264 Pope Urban IV. prescribed this feast for all Christendom.

HOW MOTHER CLARA MULTI-PLIED THE HALF-LOAF.

The holy Abbess Clara lived with her pious sisters on moderate alms. But when a famine broke out the alms stopped. Once there was only half a loaf of bread for fifty sisters. The holy abbess had it brought into the dining-hall, blessed it and broke it, into fifty pieces. All the sisters ate of it, and were satisfied. And, wonderful to relate, there was as much left as would supply as many more persons.

MOTHER CLARA PUTS A HORDE OF WARRIORS TO FLIGHT.

In the time of Mother Clara, the Emperor Frederick II. threw Italy into a state of terror. He persecuted the Pope, burned the papal cities, and plundered churches and convents. A portion of his godless army attacked the convent of

Mother Clara, and were climbing the walls. The nuns fled shrieking to the bed where Mother Clara lay sick. The mother had herself carried, bearing the Blessed Sacrament, to the convent gates. The soldiers were seized with a sudden fear. An invisible power put them to flight, and the convent was saved.

DUKE AMADEUS'S HOUNDS.

Duke Amadeus of Savoy was a most benevolent prince. A foreign ambassador once asked him if he kept many hounds for the chase. The duke replied that he would show him, if he came back the following day. When the ambassador arrived the duke led him into a room from whence he could look out into the courtyard. There he saw a long table at which a great number of poor men were eating. Amadeus said: "There are my hounds, with which in this life I chase for heaven."

The ambassador remarked, among other things, that there were many persons who would rather beg than work. Amadeus answered: "It is not for me to investigate that closely. If God were to ordain that it should be considered whether we have not rendered ourselves unworthy of His benefits by our manifold sins, He too would be forced to withdraw His generous hand."

ST. ANTHONY'S SERMON.

St. Anthony of Padua was a pious, humble monk. His mild countenance, benign look, and earnest, calm mien, made a wonderful impression on all. When he preached, the churches could not contain the throngs. One day he said to one of the brothers: "Brother, come and let us preach!" They walked silently through the streets. The brother often halted, and thought the saint would preach. Anthony, however, continued on his way, without saying a word. At last they returned to the monastery. The brother then asked the saint why he did not preach. Anthony replied: "Believe me, we have, through our modest demeanor and our earnest, serious air, preached well."

HOW THE CREATURE REVERED THE CREATOR.

AMONG the hearers of St. Anthony, on a certain occasion, was a man who denied the real presence of Christ in the Blessed Sacrament. Anthony had several conversations with this unbeliever. But he adhered to his error, and sneeringly remarked that he would not believe until he saw his ass pay reverence to the Blessed Sacrament. The saint accepted his proposition. The unbeliever kept the ass three days without food. When, however, the holy man appeared with the most

Blessed Sacrament, attended by an immense concourse of people, and the unbeliever placed plenty of food before the ass, the animal did not seem to notice it, but dropped on its fore knees when Anthony commanded it to do so in the name of God.

ST. ANTHONY PREACHES TO THE FISHES.

St. Anthony once visited Rimini to conquer by his preaching the heretics who predominated there. But nobody would listen to him. When he mounted the pulpit the obdurate heretics raised such a disturbance that he could not proceed. Whereupon the saint proceeded to the seashore, and in all simplicity cried out: "Come hither, ye fishes, and hear me, as these unbelievers will not." The fishes immediately came in swarms to the shore, and raised their heads above the water. The saint reminded them of the goodness of God, and admonished them to praise their beneficent Creator. After having blessed the fishes, they returned to the deep. Moved by this astounding miracle, several of the inhabitants of Rimini listened to the preaching of the saint, and renounced their errors.

ST. ANTHONY AND THE CHILD JESUS.

ST. ANTHONY cherished a burning love for the Mother of God, and the Child Jesus. He could never cease praising them in song, in the sweetest words, and addressing them in fervent prayer. One day the Child Jesus bowed to him, His hands embraced him, and He allowed Himself to be taken in the saint's arms. Soon after this miracle St. Anthony died, although only thirty-six years of age, worn out through his zeal in the service of God.

St. Anthony is represented with a lily in his hand and the Infant Jesus in his arms.

ST. ANTHONY'S TONGUE.

AFTER the death of St. Anthony of Padua the inhabitants built a magnificent church in honor of the great saint and miracle-worker. St. Bonaventura himself came to Padua in order to personally accompany the translation of the remains of the saint. When the saint's coffin was exhumed and opened, his body was found to have decayed, but his tongue was preserved and pure as in life. On seeing this, St. Bonaventura flung himself on his knees before the assembled multitude, and exclaimed: "O blessed tongue, which so often praised God and taught others to praise Him, it is now revealed how great thy reward is in the sight of God." The holy tongue was enshrined in a precious vessel and deposited in a chapel of the church, where it is to this day exhibited and revered.

HOW ST. ELIZABETH BECAME LANDGRAVINE.

KING ANDREW of Hungary had a very pretty daughter, four years old, named Elizabeth. When the powerful and highly esteemed Landgrave Herman of Thuringia was apprised of this, he sent a gorgeous embassy to the King of Hungary. The embassy declared their mission was to ask if the princess might be betrothed to the landgrave's son, Louis. The king and his wife gladly acceded to the request, and gave their daughter, together with many rich presents, to the ambassadors. They returned rejoicing to the castle with the princess and a number of her playmates. The landgrave and his wife received the princess with great joy and thanked God for the fulfillment of their wishes. Elizabeth was brought up with the children of the landgrave. The landgrave was delighted with her pious conduct, and loved her as if she was his own child. After his death, he was succeeded by his son Louis. In the year 1220 his marriage with Elizabeth was celebrated amid great rejoicing and display at the castle.

ST. ELIZABETH'S ROSES.

THE holy Landgravine Elizabeth was an untiring benefactress of the poor. She delighted to carry food into their hovels, and she did not shrink, when performing this charitable duty, from traveling over the roughest roads. One day, while on her pious mission, her husband met her and asked what she had under her mantle. Elizabeth jocosely replied:— "Roses." She thereby meant the fragrance of charity before God. Her husband wished to see the roses. Elizabeth smilingly threw aside her mantle, and her husband saw, instead of food for the poor, a mass of roses. In remembrance of this miracle the holy landgravine is represented bearing a bunch of roses.

HOW ST. ELIZABETH BECAME A WIDOW.

IN the year 1228, the Emperor Frederick II. undertook a crusade for the redemption of the Holy Sepulchre. Landgrave Louis, as a pious prince, also took up the cross. When Elizabeth heard of his intention she fell senseless to the ground. But when Louis impressed on her that he was going to combat the infidel in the cause of Jesus, she bowed to the will of God. She accompanied her husband to the frontier, and then returned to the castle with a sad heart. The landgrave was taken ill on the voyage to Otranto. Before his death he enjoined his faithful knights to convey the tidings of his death to his wife, and when the voyage would be completed to bear his remains home. The knights promised to carry out his desire. After his death they buried him, and sent messengers with the news of his death and his ring to his wife Elizabeth.

SUFFERINGS AND DEATH OF ST. ELIZABETH.

SCARCE had Landgrave Henry heard of his brother's death than he assumed the reins of power. The bereaved Landgravine Elizabeth was compelled to leave the castle. In the middle of winter, accompanied by her children and two faithful servants, she descended the mountain on the way to Eisenach. For a long time she sought shelter in vain, for everybody feared the wrath of the landgrave. At length, some charitable persons received her. She and her servants for a time were forced to support themselves by the labor of their hands. Finally, Bishop Egbert of Bamberg heard of the helpless condition of his relative, and gave her the Castle of Botenstein for a residence. Meantime, the knights had returned with the remains of their master. Elizabeth received the body of her husband with unspeakable grief, and had it buried in the Monastery of Reinhardsbrunn. When the faithful knights heard of the ignoble action of Landgrave Henry, they reproached him for his cruelty in unsparing terms. Henry acknowledged his fault and confessed himself ready to make reparation. Elizabeth forgave him, and asked nothing more for herself than a living. After a time, in accordance with the desire of her confessor, she left her children and faithful servants, and lived thenceforth only for God and the sick. Having reached her twenty-fourth year, she was seized with a violent fever, and died November 19, 1231.

CANONIZATION OF ST. ELIZABETH.

AFTER the death of St. Elizabeth, all the people wished to look at the face of the great servant of God. Robed in the Franciscan habit, she was buried, on the fourth day after her death, in the chapel of the hospital of which she was the foundress. The Archbishop of Mayence had all the miracles performed by Elizabeth substantiated by oath, and presented the report to Pope Gregory IX. On Whitsunday, 1235, she was solemnly enrolled in the list of saints, and her feast is celebrated on the 19th of November. Scarce had the intelligence of her canonization spread abroad, than a great concourse of people assembled in Marburg. In the presence of several bishops and princes the still undecayed body was exhumed and crowned by Emperor Frederick II. For three hundred years it was visited by countless pilgrims in the Cathedral of Marburg, until at last Landgrave Philip of Hesse broke open the coffin and robbed it. But the memory of their revered patroness is still preserved in the hearts of the Catholics of that city.

A MIRACLE BY ST. DOMINIC.

St. Dominic while on his missionary travels once arrived at the bank of a river. After reaching the other side the ferryman demanded his fee. The saint replied: "I am a poor disciple of Christ, and have neither gold nor silver. But God will reward you yet for bringing me across the stream. The ferryman, in an outburst of anger, seized the saint's cloak and shouted: "Either pay me or leave me this cloak." The saint raised his eyes toward heaven, then looked down toward the earth and pointed out to the ferryman a piece of silver lying on the ground. "My brother," he said, "here is what you demand; take it, and let me go in peace."

ANOTHER MIRACLE BY ST. DOMINIC.

WHEN St. Dominic was preaching at Toulouse a number of pilgrims, who were on their way to the tomb of St. James in Compostella, entered a small boat in the Garonne. The boat suddenly capsized, and the pilgrims were precipitated into the water. On hearing the cries of the people standing on the shore, St. Dominic came out of the neighboring church, flung himself on his knees, extended his hands in the form of a cross and prayed. He then arose, turned toward the river and cried out in a loud voice: "In the name of Jesus Christ, I command you all to come to the shore." Immediately the pilgrims who had sunk appeared, alive, above the water, and were accordingly rescued.

ORIGIN OF THE ROSARY.

WHEN St. Dominic was endeavoring to bring back to the Church the Albigenses in Italy and Spain, he found all his efforts in vain. Error and crime continued to increase around him. On contemplating this deplorable state of things he implored the assistance of the powerful help of Christians. The Queen of Heaven appeared to him during his prayer, consoled him and gave him the rosary, with the command to institute it everywhere and to preach to the people on its mysteries. Overcome with joy, the saint fulfilled the command. Immediately those who had been led into error listened to him willingly, recited the rosary with him, and returned to the fold of the Church in vast numbers. Since that time the holy rosary has spread all over Christendom, and our Holy Father Leo XIII. has recommended it as a devotion to be continually practiced.

ST. FRANCIS IN PRESENCE OF SULTAN SALADIN.

WHEN the Crusaders, for the sixth time, endeavored to rescue the Holy Sepulchre in Jerusalem, from the hands of the infidels, St. Francis, who had yearned for a martyr's death, joined the Christian army. When in Egypt, he fearlessly presented himself in the very strongholds of the infidels. There he was derided, beaten and carried, bound in chains, into the presence of the sultan. The sultan asked him whence he came and by whom he had been sent. Francis courageously answered that the Almighty had sent him to point out to him and his people the true road to salvation. And then he preached with such effect the doctrine of Jesus as Christ, the Saviour of the world, that the sultan was amazed. Francis offered, as a proof of the truth of the doctrine he preached, to walk through a consuming fire. The sultan bestowed on him valuable gifts, which, however, the saint declined. Thereupon the sultan recommended himself to his prayers, and had him conveyed back to the Christian encampment unhurt and unbound.

ST. FRANCIS AND THE POOR.

On a certain occasion the brothers presented a new mantle to St. Francis. Just then a poor man came in, and in tearful accents informed the saint that his wife had died and left him with several helpless children. The saint immediately gave him his cloak, and said to him, as he presented it: "Take it, but do not give it to any one who does not pay you a high price for it." The brothers wished to regain possession of the mantle, but they had to buy it at a dear figure, and the poor man was thus relieved.

ST. FRANCIS AND THE CHRISTMAS CRIB.

IN countless Catholic churches and houses, on Christmas Eve, Christmas cribs, made of wood, or moss-covered stones, are constructed. On this beautiful festival one sees the City of Jerusalem and the country surrounding Jerusalem and Bethlehem. In the stall Mary and Joseph are kneeling, together with the shepherds, engaged in adoration. Above are the holy angels rejoicing. In the fields the shepherds are tending their flocks. On the occasion of the festival of the New Year, likewise, the Temple of Jerusalem, the High Priest, and the Circumcision of Christ may be seen On the feast of the Epiphany the three holy kings come with their servants and beasts to the stall. The three holy kings kneel before the Infant Jesus, contemplate the Divine Babe in adoration, and offer Him gold, myrrh and frankincense. Young and old rejoice on witnessing this beautiful and consoling representation. St. Francis, who so ardently loved the Infant Jesus, was the first to institute the Christmas crib. Since then it has spread over all Christendom.

KING LOUIS OF FRANCE VOWS TO UNDERTAKE A CRUSADE.

St. Louis of France was once prostrated by a severe illness. One of his servants had covered his face with a cloth, believing him dead. A servant standing on the other side of the bed asserted, on the contrary, that he was not dead. The king finally recovered. The first thing he asked for was the cross worn by those who promised to participate in the crusades. After his recovery the Bishop of Paris endeavored to persuade him to obtain from the Pope a dispensation from his vow, inasmuch as, when he made it, he was not in the full possession of his understanding, owing to the ordeal of illness through which he had passed. Louis took the cross from his shoulder and handed it to the bishop. He then requested the bishop to return it to him, saying: "Now, I take it once more, so that everybody may know that I do it in full possession of my senses."

CHIVALROUS ACT OF ST. LOUIS.

WHEN King Louis, during his first crusade, had conquered the city of Damietta, in Egypt, he marched further inland with his army. Owing to the overpowering heat and the want of food, the army endured intense suffering, and, in addition, several thousand men were swept away by a violent plague. Thus weakened, the king's army was defeated by the Saracens, the king himself was taken prisoner, and was set free only after surrendering Damietta and promising a ransom of a million pieces of gold. After the money had been brought from France, the king sent Count Montfort to deliver it to the Saracens. When the count returned he informed the king that the Saracens, in counting the coin, had made a mistake of 20,000 pieces in his majesty's favor, and that he was careful not to direct their attention to the error. The king immediately ordered the count to return the sum in question to his enemies.

DEATH OF KING LOUIS.

When King Louis had returned to France, after his unfortunate crusade, he still continued to grieve night and day over the condition of the Holy Land. He even feared lest the Christian name would be completely wiped out in Palestine, and he accordingly determined to undertake another crusade. Having made all the necessary preparations, he set sail, and landed in Tunis. It was during the heated term, and to a dearth of water were added the horrors of the plague which suddenly broke out in his army. So many died that the survivors could not bury them. The king himself was finally stricken down. The day before his death, he received the Viaticum, kneeling on the ground, despite his failing strength. With his dying breath he prayed aloud for his people and his army. Having slept for a while, he suddenly cried out: "Jerusalem! Jerusalem! we are going to Jerusalem!" As his last moments drew near he ordered his attendants to place him on a sack strewn with ashes. With hands folded across his heart, and eyes turned heavenward, St. Louis, the pious king and faithful servant of God, passed to his reward.

ST. NOTBURGA, A SERVANT.

St. Notburga served as a kitchen maid in Rottenburg Castle, Tyrol. Her noble mistress allowed her to distribute to the poor who thronged before the gates all the victuals that remained after each meal. The pious girl utilized this opportunity to instruct the poor with the word of God, while alleviating their bodily wants. The master's son married a woman named Ottila. She was of a miserly disposition, and was angry at seeing Notburga giving the remains of the daily victuals to the poor.

While the old people lived, she dared not offer any opposition, but after their death she ordered the servant maid to give the remnants of the meals to the hogs, instead of the poor. Notburga accordingly saved a portion of her own meals for the needy standing at the gates. This noble action of the servant incensed her heartless mistress. She complained to her husband that Notburga's immoderate generosity attracted a riff-raff crowd before the gates, and added that such conduct constituted a grave danger, when the master should be absent from the castle. She accordingly dismissed her with the consent of her husband.

ST. Notburga also served some time with a farmer in the Tyrol. Her agreement was that she should cease work on the eve of every Sunday or Holyday, as soon as the Angelus was rung. One evening during the harvest she wished to retire to the neighboring chapel, when the Angelus bell sounded, to perform her usual devotions. The farmer wished her to continue at work for some time longer. Notburga replied: "My sickle will determine my right." She flung her sickle in the air, where it remained hanging, to the amazement of the farmer and his help. Hence St. Notburga is represented with a sickle in her hand.

SIMPLICITY OF ST. JOHN OF KANTI.

ST. JOHN OF KANTI was a priest and professor in Cracow. On a certain occasion he made a journey to Rome, on foot and alone, as was his wont. He was attacked by robbers on the way, who threatened him with death unless he surrendered his money to them. In the excitement John forgot that he had stowed away in his clothes a few pieces of gold, as a provision for the journey, and he accordingly declared that he had given up everything he possessed. When the robbers had retired he remembered for the first time the money he had concealed on his person. He at once hastened after them. When he had overtaken them, he fell on his knees and confessed that he had told an untruth, and begged God's pardon. At the same time he handed them the money. The robbers were amazed at such simplicity and innocence. Their callous souls were touched and melted like ice before the sun. They threw themselves at the feet of the holy man, begged his pardon, and restored to him all they had taken from him.

ST. CATHERINE OF SIENNA AND POPE GREGORY XI.

ST. CATHERINE OF SIENNA lived at the time when the Popes had left Rome on account of the disturbances that then prevailed, and had temporarily taken up their residence at Avignon. This removal of the Vicar of Christ from the graves of the holy apostles Peter and Paul had already lasted seventy years. At length the Roman people turned to St. Catherine and besought her to bring about the return of Pope Gregory to Rome. The saint accordingly set out for Avignon, and was received by the Pope with great honor. The Pope had made a vow to return to Rome, but he dared not then fulfill it on account of his fear of the French king. St. Catherine had known, through a revelation, this vow of the Holy Father, and she said to him: "Do what you have promised God to do." The

Pope, surprised at these words, followed the advice of the saint, and returned to Rome in the year 1376.

ST. BERNARDINE AS A YOUTH.

ST. BERNARDINE belonged to a distinguished family of Sienna. In his youth he was a model of innocence. When his companions engaged in objectionable conversation or sports, they immediately ceased as soon as Bernardine approached. When he had grown to manhood a pestilence broke out in Sienna. All those who attended the sick were stricken down, and the victims were left to die without care, Then it was that Bernardine resolved to devote himself to the care of the sick. with a number of his friends. His relations objected vehemently to this, inasmuch as he would place his life in danger and entail disgrace on his family by engaging in such a common calling. But Bernardine was not to be dissuaded from his purpose. He continued to serve the sick for four months, until the plague subsided.

BERNARDINE OF SIENNA AS A PREACHER.

ST. BERNARDINE, when a youth, sold his property, gave the proceeds to the poor, and entered the Order of St. Francis. After a time his superior appointed him official preacher. He had the holy name of Jesus engraved on a tablet, and surrounded by golden rays. This tablet he carried with him into the pulpit; he showed it to the people, and preached with fervent zeal on the holy name of Jesus. The people, swayed by his intense eloquence, cast themselves at his feet, and joyously hailed the saving sign of salvation. And so he went from city to city and brought back whole communities to the fold of Christ.

The most bitter enemies were reconciled; the usurers restored their ill-gotten gains; the gambling-tables were deserted and the follies of fashion disappeared. The enemies of Bernardine misrepresented his preaching to the Pope. But Bernardine soon vindicated himself. The Pope twice offered him the episcopal dignity. But he preferred to remain a simple Franciscan. He healed multitudes through the holy sign of the cross. He was consumed by his zeal for the honor of God and the salvation of souls. He preached for the last time at Ricti. When dying, he ordered that he should be laid on the pavement of his cell, where he received the Most Holy Sacrament. With his arms folded on his breast, and his eyes raised toward heaven, he passed away, April 20, 1444. He is represented in the Franciscan habit, with the holy name of Jesus in his hand.

RELEASING THE CAPTIVES.

SEVEN centuries ago the Mohammedans were pirates along the African shores of the Mediterranean. They captured Christian vessels and sold the Christians as slaves in their markets. Filled with compassion for these unhappy victims of barbarism, St. John of Matha entered the Order for the Ransom of Captives. He traveled to Tunis and ransomed as many captives as his accumulated collections allowed. St. John strengthened the others in the Christian faith, and comforted them with the promise of speedy freedom. When on one occasion he had embarked with 120 slaves, the infidels cut his sails and left him to the mercy of the waves. But John did not lose courage. He converted the garments of his companions into sails, knelt with the crucifix in his hand, and chanted psalms during the remainder of the voyage. The vessel landed the ransomed captives in their own country without having encountered the slightest mishap.

PIETY OF ST. THOMAS AQUINAS.

ST. THOMAS AQUINAS was one of the greatest divines ever enlightened by the Holy Ghost. When, in accordance with the order of his superior, he mounted the pulpit as preacher, no hall could contain the multitudes that thronged to hear him. He was accustomed to say, however, that he had learned less from the books than he had learned at the foot of the crucifix. And for this Jesus rewarded him in a most striking manner. When Thomas one day was praying before the crucifix in the chapel of the Dominican convent in Naples, he was seen by a brother monk to be miraculously lifted from the ground. This brother heard to his great amazement these words uttered to St. Thomas from the cross:

"You have written well of Me, Thomas; what reward do you ask of Me?" The saint simply answered: "Nothing else than Thyself, O Lord!"

ST. EDWARD THE CONFESSOR.

THE Holy Scriptures tell us we should not put our trust in princes. But many princes, under the influence of the Catholic Church, have been the best of men. Among these was Edward the Confessor, of England. St. Edward devoted his whole life to the benefaction of his fellow-men. He hated all evils, and opposed them in every form. His great ambition was to found his life on the basis of virtue. He was much devoted to prayer, to visiting churches and sustaining the cause of true religion. He possessed nearly all the moral virtues, but he was especially distinguished by his spirit of piety. Ambition had no place in his soul.

St. Edward fulfilled the commands of God in all things. He protected the rights of the Church and the liberties of his people with scrupulous care, and had no other ambition than the comfort of his distressed subjects. He, on one occasion, declared he would not accept the greatest monarchy if it cost the life of a single man. The saint was always opposed to war. He restored Malcolm, King of Scotland, and in his charity he even opposed a proposed massacre of the Danes who had wantonly invaded England. He was noted for his liberal alms, and he called the money gathered into his exchequer "a pillaging of the poor." He never talked of vanity or pleasure, as kings generally do, but of God and His spiritual dominion. Humility, prayer and mortification were the ruling principles of his life. He was singularly devoted to the Blessed Virgin and the Holy Family, and devoted, as St. Aldred tells us, to a vow of perpetual chastity. In everything connected with the Church he was a saintly model; and even yet the English Catholics congregate around his tomb in Westminster Abbey and offer up prayers to God in his name.

ST. JOHN OF CAPISTRANO AND THE HUSSITES.

St. John of Capistrano was a great preacher and miracle-worker. Even the most hardened sinners yielded to his words. On this account Pope Nicholas V. sent him to Germany to combat the Hussite heresy. The saint succeeded in bringing back many thousands to the Catholic Church. His enemies accordingly resolved to destroy his reputation through artifice. At Breslau they placed a young man in a coffin. They then brought him, in the presence of a great multitude of people, to the saint, and asked him, with feigned sorrow, to restore the dead man to life. The saint exclaimed before the people: "This man is dead forever." This was a signal for a burst of derisive laughter on the part of the Hussites. One of them approached the coffin and said: "Peter, I say to you, arise!" But the young man was dead, and never rose again.

ST. JOHN'S POWER OVER THE ELEMENTS.

ST. JOHN OF CAPISTRANO preached on one occasion in Mortegno to a great assemblage in the open field. During the sermon heavy storm-clouds gathered overhead. The skies grew dark, and the people began to grow apprehensive, in view of the approaching storm. But, desirous of hearing the word of God, nobody left the place. John offered up a brief prayer with the people, and behold! while the rain fell in torrents all around them, the ground on which the preacher and the people stood did not receive a drop. The inhabitants of the town begged the saint to give them, in remembrance of this miracle, the cloak which he wore. They received it, and they declare to this day that they are indebted to this relic for many favors and blessings.

JOHN OF CAPISTRANO, THE COURAGEOUS MONK.

WHEN JOHN OF CAPISTRANO was engaged in preaching in Germany and Poland, the terrible news arrived that Constantinople had fallen into the hands of the Sultan Mohammed. After the capture of this city the proud conqueror contemplated the subjection of all Christendom to the Turkish power. The Pope, foreseeing the danger that threatened Christendom, was sad at heart, but, guided by Providence, perceived that the Turks should be resisted and thrown back. His Holiness, therefore, sent the renowned preacher and miracle-worker, St. John of Capistrano, to the parliamentary assembly at Neustadt. John preached to the assembled princes with such enthusiasm that they unanimously agreed to fight the enemies of Christianity with all the power at their command. The saint performed a like service at Raab, in presence of the Hungarian magnates. The Hungarian Regent, Hunyad, marched at the head of his army, accompanied by the saint, against the Turks, who had beleaguered Belgrade by land and water. With the banner of St. Bernardine in hand, the Christian monk fired the warriors to battle. He prostrated himself on his knees, like a second Moses, raised his arms to heaven in prayer, and then arose and led the Christian army to where the hottest conflict prevailed. The Turks fought with great fury to capture Belgrade. They burst through the battered walls into the city. Hunyad, for the moment, lost courage. But at this critical moment the saint cried out: "This is the day that God has appointed for our victory." And as he spoke, he dashed on the Turkish positions with several thousand men. The Turkish forces were thrown into confusion by this vehement charge. They fled in dismay, some of them being cut down by the sword, while others were drowned by plunging into the river. The Christians reaped an immense booty. After Hunyad and Capistrano had offered up their thanksgiving for this plain aid of Providence, they conveyed the intelligence of their great victory to Pope Calixtus. Overjoyed at this glorious news, the Pope ordered that the religious celebration of this event should be solemnized on the feast of the Transfiguration of Christ.

LOUIS XI. AND FRANCIS OF PAULA.

THE powerful King Louis XI. fell sick, and no physician could afford him relief. He sent messengers with many valuable gifts to Francis, asking the saint to come and help him. But Francis would neither accept the gifts nor repair to the royal palace. The king therefore had recourse to the King of Naples in order that the latter might induce the saint to undertake the journey. But the saint refused even then to set out on a journey of four hundred miles to enable a prince to cling for a few brief years to the world and to life. But King Louis persisted, and finally appealed to the Pope. Francis could not disobey the voice of the head of the Church, and set out on his journey. The king went out to meet him, and begged for his assistance. St. Francis answered: "We must, O King, give ourselves up to the will of God. In His hands are life and death. Little more of life remains to you; you must make such preparations as death demands." The king ordered a dwelling to be given the saint, with all the furnishings and necessaries of life on a luxurious scale. The saint refused to accept them. The king then sent him a picture of the Mother of God, made of pure gold, together with a purse of ducats, for the purpose of building a monastery. These the saint likewise sent back, with the following words: "It were better the king would restore his ill-gotten goods than give them away in alms." Finally the prayers and admonitions of Francis were effectual; the king made reparation for his offenses, and died repentant.

ST. FRANCIS COMMANDS THE ELEMENTS.

ST. FRANCIS OF PAULA was obliged on one occasion to go to the Island of Sicily, and sailed accompanied by Brother Thomas. The captain refused to carry unknown men without first having been paid the passage money. Thereupon the saint fell on his knees and prayed. He then arose, fastened Brother Thomas's cloak to his staff, and threw his own mantle on the water. They both embarked on the mantle, and the wind drove them forward. They came up with the ship on the high seas. The ship's crew were overcome with wonder, and invited them to enter the vessel. But the saint, trusting in God, kept on his way, and finally reached Sicily.

HOW ST. NICHOLAS OF THE FLUE INSURED PEACE.

FOUR hundred years ago the Swiss League held a meeting at Stanz. Instead, however, of agreeing in regard to the affairs of their fatherland, violent dissensions arose. There were angry speeches delivered, and it looked as if civil war would be the result. At this juncture the hermit Nicholas entered, barefooted and bareheaded, wearing a long cloak and carrying a staff in his hand. All arose to do him reverence, and listened in silence and curiosity to hear what he had to say. The hermit advocated peace and unity with such earnestness and eloquence that in an hour all difficulties were settled and each member of the league was bearing to his home the happy news of union and peace. In all the cities and towns joy-bells were rung, and the preservation of peace was celebrated amid general rejoicings.

ST. THOMAS OF VILLANOVA.

St. Thomas evinced, when a child, a wonderful pleasure in giving alms. When going to school he usually gave his dinner to the first beggar he met. He came home several times without shoes, stockings or coat. The money and victuals which he received from his parents he gave to the poor and sick. On one occasion he was at home alone and the key of the money-chest was not to be found. As several poor people were congregated at the door, he took six young chickens and divided them among them. When his mother reproached him for his action, he replied: "The sight of the poor people excited my compassion. If another one had come, I would have given him the old hen too, rather than let him go away empty-handed."

ST. THOMAS OF VILLANOVA AS ARCHBISHOP.

When St. Thomas of Villanova was appointed Archbishop of Valencia, his beneficence knew no bounds. What he derived from his bishopric and received in presents was all given to the poor. He wore for many years when archbishop the identical habit he wore when an humble monk. He followed the same rule in the matter of victuals as he did in regard to clothes. His butler was once compelled to return to market with a dear fish he had purchased. The archbishop preferred to give the money to the poor, instead of expending it on costly eatables. Almost every day a vast throng of beggars assembled before his gate. Each received a plate of soup, a drink of wine, and a little money. The instructions of the archbishop to his butler were: "Give to all, give kindly and with a good heart." When he died 8,000 beggars accompanied this great friend of the poor to his grave, with tears and lamentations.

GENEROSITY OF THE BLESSED JORDAN.

THE Blessed Jordan was General of the Dominicans. He once met on the street a man who complained that he was ill, and asked for alms. The saint had no money, but gave him some clothing. The man disposed of the clothing at a tavern. A brother remarked this, and told Jordan of the evil that had emanated from his charitable action. The latter answered: "Generosity commands a man to give to one who appears to be poor or sick. I prefer to have lost the clothing I gave him rather than to have lost my generosity."

ST. IGNATIUS OF LOYOLA.

St. Ignatius, the founder of the glorious Society of Jesus, so famous for its achievements in the conversion of barbaric peoples, the diffusion of learning, the advancement of science, and the defense of Catholicity against the adherents of the religious rebellion of the sixteenth century, was born of a noble family in 1491, in the Castle of Loyola, Biscay, Spain. In his youth he was page to Ferdinand V. He afterward adopted the military profession, and while in the army behaved with marked bravery. During this period of his life he was distinguished by his excellent conduct and noble and generous disposition. At the battle of Pampeluna, he received a severe wound, and during his convalescence he passed much of his time in reading the lives of our Saviour and of the Saints, which were the only books at hand. He was so impressed with the sacrifices of these heroic servants of God, that he resolved to devote his life to His service.

"One night," says his latest biographer, "being prostrate before an image of the Blessed Virgin, he consecrated himself to the service of his Redeemer, under her patronage, and vowed an inviolable fidelity. When he had ended his prayer he heard a great noise; the house shook, the windows of his chambers were broken, and a rent made in the walls, which remains to this day. Another night, Ignatius saw the Mother of God, environed with light, holding the Infant Jesus in her arms. This vision replenished his soul with spiritual delight, and made all sensual pleasure and worldly objects insipid to him ever after."

Shortly after he retired to the Convent of Mansesa, where he wrote his wonderful book of "Spiritual Exercises."* After countless trials and difficulties, Ignatius was joined by a few devoted companions, among them Peter Faber, James Laynez, and St. Francis Xavier, and determined to institute the "Society of Jesus," which project was approved by Pope Paul III., September 27, 1540. Hence we see that one of the greatest of religious organizations ever founded originated in the reading of pious books.

ST. FRANCIS XAVIER.

ST. FRANCIS XAVIER, the Apostle of the Indies, was the first to introduce Christianity among the dense pagan populations of the East. His labors in Hindoostan, Malacca and Japan, for a period of twelve years, were more successful than those of any missionary of modern times.

---

* An English translation of this book is published by J. Schaefer, 60 Barclay street, New York.

After he had preached in the Indies, he desired to win China also to the Church of Christ. With three other Jesuit fathers he voyaged on a Portuguese merchant vessel. After a long and dangerous voyage the vessel landed at the Isle of Sanacian, which was held by the Portuguese as a trading-place. The saint anxiously waited for the ship to proceed on its way. But as the vessel was delayed he was deeply chagrined over the result of this voyage. He was so prostrated with fever that he could no longer stand erect. The saint now knew that his last hour was approaching. On December 2d, 1552, he breathed his last on this lonely isle. His body was buried there, but was removed to Goa two years afterward. His arm, with which he had baptized a hundred thousand persons and wrought countless miracles, is in Rome. Pope Gregory X. enrolled him in the list of the saints. He is represented in the habit of his order, lying sick on a straw mat, with the crucifix pressed to his bosom and his eyes looking heavenward.

HIS MIRACLES.

He was especially endowed by Almighty God with the gift of working miracles, in order to draw the benighted heathen to the fold of Christ.

On one occasion, while preaching at Manapar, messengers arrived asking him to come and cure their master, who was possessed of a devil. Not wishing to interrupt his instructions, he took from his breast a small cross, and giving it to some of his little convert children, bade them go and perform the miracle. The children hastened to the presence of the afflicted man, and induced him to kiss the cross. Immediately the Evil One was expelled, and a multitude of persons who witnessed the power of the cross renounced their idolatry and requested to be baptized. On another occasion, Anthony Miranda, one of his catechists, while sleeping in his tent, was bitten by a cobra snake, whose sting is certain death. In the morning the dead youth's companion hastened to the saint and in tearful accents told him what had occurred. St. Francis hurried to the spot, knelt by the dead body, offered up a brief prayer, touched the wounded limb with his spittle, and exclaimed: "Anthony, in the name of Jesus Christ, arise!" The dead youth immediately arose, and resumed his journey as if nothing had happened. Again, while sailing from Malacca to the Chinese coast, the son of a Moor, five years of age, fell overboard. The father was beside himself with grief. St. Francis knew nothing of the accident for several days after, when, meeting the father, he inquired the cause of his trouble. "Supposing," said the saint, "Almighty God were to bring your child back again to the ship, alive and well, would you promise to believe in Him and to become a Christian?" The disconsolate parent immediately promised. Three days afterward the child was seen sitting in the same spot from which he had fallen into the sea. He could give no account of himself since the moment of his disappearance. In remembrance of so great a favor the overjoyed father had his son baptized by the name of Francis. The countless miracles accomplished by this great Apostle were always performed in the presence of multitudes, and are incontrovertibly authenticated.

ST. STANISLAUS KOSTKA.

St. Stanislaus Kostka is an illustrious model of youthful piety. He was born in Poland, of a distinguished family, October 28, 1550. From his earliest youth he was devoted to meditation and prayer, and often during the latter exercise he would fall into raptures, while torrents of tears would gush from his eyes. While pursuing his studies, his brother, who was two years older than himself, repeatedly beat and abused him, as he regarded Stanislaus's pious conduct a reproach to his own evil manner of living. Stanislaus died in his seventeenth year, and was canonized by Benedict XIII. in 1727, after several miracles by him had been manifestly authenticated. One of these occurred in 1674, in Lima, Peru, the truth of which was attested by five eminent physicians, a surgeon, and all of the Jesuits. A novice in the convent was deprived by palsy of all physical motion, so that he could not stir hand or foot. The affliction was aggravated by symptoms of other diseases, so that the physicians pronounced him incurable. A picture of the saint was, on his feast, November 13, applied to the palsied one's side; feeling was restored, and the sufferer immediately recovered his health.

ST. TERESA OF JESUS.

ST. TERESA was born in Avila, Spain, March 28, 1515. Her parents were of distinguished descent, and noted for their piety. They brought up their children in the way of virtue, taking special care to mould their minds in early youth. Teresa was endowed with a susceptible and ardent nature. She was fond of reading the Lives of the Saints when yet quite young, and their sufferings and their virtues stimulated her to tread the path of perfection. In her twelfth year she lost her mother, after which she chose Our Blessed Lady to take the place of a mother to her.

In her twentieth year she joined the Order of Mitigated Carmelites, at Avila.

Before taking this step she had spent much time in anxious deliberation, and finally reasoned thus: "The trials and sufferings of living as a nun cannot be greater than the pains of Purgatory, and I have well deserved to be in hell. It is not much to spend the rest of my life as if I were in Purgatory, and then go straight to Heaven." For some time after her admission as a nun she was prostrated by severe bodily suffering, which she bore unmurmuringly, until she at last obtained her cure through the intercession of St. Joseph. One day, on entering the chapel, she fixed her eyes on a picture representing the Passion of Our Lord. Reflecting on His sufferings for us, and on her own ingratitude, she prostrated herself before the picture, and in a passion of tears implored that she should never offend her Saviour again. Her prayer was granted. "From that moment," she writes, I opened a new book—that is, I began a new life. The life I had hitherto lived was my own; but that which I have lived since, I may say, has been God's, for, as it seems to me, God has lived in me."

St. Teresa cherished a special devotion to the Most Holy Sacrament, and when permitted by her confessor, communicated every day. A story is told of her which illustrates her patience and meekness. She was kneeling one day in a church in Toledo, where she was occupied at the time in the establishment of a convent. She was muffled up in a cloak in an obscure corner of the church. A woman, who had lost one of her pattens, seeing the muffled form, concluded that was the culprit, and approaching her, gave her a violent slap with the remaining patten, and demanded back the missing one. Teresa protested, but in vain. Her angry assailant would not listen, but proceeded to give her several smart blows on the head. When the people came to her rescue, Teresa simply remarked, with a smile: "Heaven preserve the good woman! Just as if my headache had not been bad enough before she began!" And she quietly continued her devotions.

ST. ALOYSIUS GONZAGA.

ST. ALOYSIUS GONZAGA was born in the Castle of Castiglione, Northern Italy, March 9, 1568. His father, Ferdinand, was Prince of the Holy Roman Empire, Marquis of Castiglione, and Lord Chamberlain to the King of Spain. His mother was Lady Martha de Santena, a Spanish noblewoman. In his fourth year Aloysius was taken by his father into camp, where he remained for a while, but on the embarkation of the troops for Tunis he was sent back to his mother. The pious woman was overwhelmed with grief on hearing the disedifying expressions he had picked up in camp from the soldiers. He ever afterward looked back on this comparatively harmless episode as the great sin of his life, and when he made his first confession he fainted at the priest's feet, through the intensity of grief in accusing himself of it. Never after did he commit a deliberate sin, either mortal or venial.

As he grew older, the practice of the virtue of chastity became his ambition. God was pleased with this holy desire on the part of His servant, and hence we find Aloysius, when only in his tenth year, kneeling in the Chapel of the Annunciation at Florence, his soul aglow with divine love, devoting himself to God and the ever-pure Virgin by a vow of perpetual chastity. From this time on his life was a continued advance in heroic sanctity. Converse with his Creator and Lord became his constant delight, and his very breathing was the exhalation of prayer. He received his first communion from the hands of the illustrious St. Charles Borromeo. Ever afterward it was his custom to receive the Holy of Holies every Sunday and Holyday. He always devoted three days for preparation and three for thanksgiving. About a year later Aloysius accompanied his parents to the Court of King Philip of Spain, where both he and his brother were appointed pages of the heir of the Spanish throne. But the gairish glitter of court life had little attraction for Aloysius. His whole mind was absorbed in the one work of advancing in holiness. He began to make it a rule, when any new project was proposed, to question himself thus: "Aloysius, how will this advance the attainment of eternal life?" If the matter were worth doing from that point of view, he did it; if not, he let it alone.

Finally, Aloysius determined to join the Society of Jesus, which then had not been long established. In this he met with vehement opposition from his father. Every means was adopted to shake the boy's constancy (he was then only fifteen years of age), but in vain. This cruel martyrdom lasted three years. He meantime redoubled his former austerities, so much so that his father and all his relatives concluded, if his life was to be spared, he should be allowed to place himself under the prudent control of spiritual obedience. He therefore renounced his title and heirdom in favor of his brother Ralph, and, on the 25th of November, 1585, in the eighteenth year of his age, entered the Society of Jesus, of which he became one of the most glorious ornaments.

MORTIFICATION OF ST. ALOYSIUS.

The mortifications practiced by St. Aloysius were hardly credible. Not being in the way of procuring the simple instruments of penance in use among religious communities, he invented some of his own. For lack of an ordinary discipline, he made a scourge out of seven leathern straps; in these he fastened sharp nails and fragments of broken iron chain, and with this cruel weapon he daily scourged his naked shoulders so that the walls and floor of his room were bespattered with his blood.

Instead of the ordinary spiked chain (Catinella) which penitents are wont to wear around their loins, he devised a cincture studded with the rowels of old riding-spurs, and girt himself therewith. He strewed his mattress with little blocks of wood, that he might lie uneasily. On

Wednesdays he abstained from meat; on Fridays, in honor of our Lord's Passion, he fed only on bread and water; and on Saturdays fasted in like manner in honor of the Blessed Virgin. These are merely given as some specimens of his penitential ingenuity. Thirsting to partake in the sufferings of Christ, grieving over the sins of others, longing to make reparation for the ingratitude of men, he treated himself as if he were the vilest criminal.

DEATH OF ST. ALOYSIUS.

EVEN the shadows of death were bright to Aloysius. Seven months before he died, while he was staying at the Jesuit House in Milan, it was revealed to him, as he made his morning meditation, that he had but a short time to live. He received this divine intimation with rapturous delight. Meantime he studied diligently, and his free time was devoted to preaching in the public squares, catechising children and visiting the sick in hospitals. He likewise succeeded in making peace between the rival branches of his own family, who were engaged in a fierce dispute, which had resulted in open violence. Above all, he had the happiness of converting his younger and somewhat unprincipled brother, saving him from a great crime and preventing a grievous scandal.

He was most tenderly devoted to the Sacred Heart of Jesus. This fact is noteworthy, inasmuch as this devotion had not yet been authorized by the Church. In 1591 a deadly pestilence broke out in Rome, and as the accommodation in the hospitals was insufficient, the Jesuits built one at their own expense and served it themselves. Even the General of the Order constituted himself a nurse. Several of the Fathers died martrys of charity on this occasion. It was, of course, a harvest time for Aloysius. One day he found a poor fever-stricken creature dying in the street. The passers-by, afraid of infection, kept at a distance. Aloysius, without hesitation, took the sick man up, and carried him on his back to the hospital. He caught the infection, and after four months of patient suffering resigned his soul to God, in his twenty-third year, June 21, 1591. No less than two thousand three hundred and forty-five miracles were offered in evidence at the process of the canonization of St. Aloysius.

THE BLESSED PETER CANISIUS.

AMONG the men who were instrumental in preserving the Catholic faith in Germany and Switzerland, Father Canisius holds a foremost place. For many years he went as a missionary from city to city and town to town. All classes thronged to listen to his preaching. After his sermons he would often hear confessions till late in the night. Thousands of people who, through the false teachings of Luther, Zwingli and Calvin, had grown indifferent, were strengthened by him in the faith, and many who had entirely fallen away were brought back to the Church. He accordingly incurred the anger of the heretics, who lost no occasion to insult and injure him, and who even sought his life. Canisius also greatly improved the high schools for Catholic students, and published an excellent catechism for the people. He combated the destructive doctrines of the time by his wise counsels to the Pope, the German emperor, several German princes, and the Government of the Canton of Freiburg. After having labored untiringly over fifty years for the honor of God and the advancement of the Church, Canisius died, in his seventy-seventh year, at Freiburg, Switzerland, December 21, 1597.

MISSIONARY LABORS AND MARTYRDOM OF ST. FIDELIS IN GRANBUENDEN.

ST. FIDELIS OF SIGMARINGEN was in early life a lawyer. When thirty-four years of age he entered the Capuchin order. On account of his saintly life and great eloquence, he was appointed by Papal brief missionary preacher to the Calvinists of Granbuenden. He entered on his apostolic mission in the depth of winter. He traveled, barefooted and clothed in the poorest garments, from city to city, and ascended the pulpit exhausted, hungry, cold. After his wearisome labors his only refreshment, as a rule, was a piece of bread which he had begged, while his bed consisted of a little hay in a stable. The return of the Calvinists of Granbuenden to the bosom of the Catholic Church increased daily. Enraged at this, the Calvinist preachers incited the fanatical peasantry against Fidelis. While preaching at Sevis he was shot at in the pulpit, but his would-be assassin missed his aim. Scarcely had Fidelis left the church when a crowd of blasphemous swearers and uproarious men gathered around him. One struck him with a sword, and others beat him with cudgels. At last, one fanatic hit him on the head with a club and fractured his skull, and the saint in a few minutes was dead.

MARY, HELP OF CHRISTIANS.

In the time of Pope Pius V., the Turks were the rulers of the seas. They robbed the Christians of their commercial vessels, and led thousands into slavery. The great object of the Pope, at that crisis, was to check the arch-enemy of the Christian name and punish him for his outrages. He united the Spanish and Venetian fleets against the invaders. He sent ambassadors to the German emperor, to the kings of France and Poland, and the Italian princes, imploring their aid against the common enemy. He placed the Christian fleet under the protection of the Queen of Heaven, and ordered that prayers should be offered up for her intercession throughout all Christendom. On October 7, 1571, the famous battle of Lepanto was fought, when the Christians won a decisive victory over the Turks. At the moment of the battle the Pope was engaged in work with the Cardinals. He opened the window, looked heavenward and cried: "No more business; only thanks to God for the great victory He has accorded to the Christians at this moment." In memory of this glorious event, the Pope caused the feast of the rosary to be celebrated on the first

Sunday in October. He also had inserted in the Litany of the Blessed Virgin the invocation, "Help of Christians, pray for us."

ST. ROSE OF LIMA.

ST. ROSE OF LIMA is one of the few canonized saints of the New World. She was born in the city of Lima in 1586. From her earliest childhood she was given to practices of piety, and was a model of virtue to all who came near her. Her baptismal name was Isabel, but her sweetness of disposition and beautiful countenance won for her the title of Rose, by which she was ever afterward known. Frail of body, she suffered greatly in her youth, but she bore her pains with heroic Christian fortitude. She worked hard, despite her weakness and suffering, to support her parents, who were poor. She subjected herself to the severest austerities. Beneath her habit she wore a coarse hair-cloth, and she bore a silver crown on her head, set with sharp points. She cherished an intense devotion to the Most Blessed Sacrament, and spent many hours in its presence, both night and day. The tercentenary of this holy servant of God was celebrated in the year 1886 in the city of Lima with great splendor, all classes of civil society, from the highest functionary to the humblest citizen, uniting with the ecclesiastical authorities in honoring her memory. The festival lasted three days.

ST. FELIX OF CANTALICIO AND THE JUDGE.

St. Felix of Cantalicio was a poor Capuchin in Rome. For forty years he was engaged in begging for his brethren. Poorly clad, barefooted, with a bag on his back and the rosary in his hand, he went from door to door begging for his order. On one occasion he came into the presence of a judge who had been presented with a calf. The calf began to bawl. Felix laughingly said to the judge: "Do you understand the language of that calf? If not, I can tell you. The calf simply demands a favorable verdict for the one who made a present of it to you. Be careful to do nothing against your conscience, so that on the day of judgment such gifts will not be for your perdition." The judge was struck at these words, and returned the calf to the donor.

ST. CHARLES BORROMEO.

St. Charles Borromeo, when Archbishop of Milan, was accustomed to visit the most outlying parishes of his diocese. One day he arrived at a swollen stream that flowed from the Alps. The passageway was swept off, and the saint stood helpless on the shore. A robust mountaineer proposed to carry him across on his shoulders. In the midst of the waves, however, he lost his balance, and the archbishop tumbled into the water. The carrier now only cared for his own safety. When he reached the shore, in his excitement he ran away. The archbishop battled with the waves for a time, and finally reached the shore. . Dripping with water, he arrived in a quarter of an hour at a house where he dried his garments. The carrier also sought refuge at the same time in the same house. The saint did not upbraid him, but, on the contrary, spoke to him in a friendly manner, encouraged him, and gave him some money.

WHY DUKE FRANCIS OF BORGIA BECAME A JESUIT.

CHARLES V. once held at Toledo a great meeting of his nobles. With the magnificence only possible to a great ruler whose sway extended over half the world, he kept up a continued round of festivities. But in the midst of the rejoicings the empress suddenly fell ill of a fever. Excitement reigned all around. The festivities ceased. Processions and devotions of various kinds were held, but in a few days the beloved empress died. Duke Francis of Borgia, as high lord of the court, was commanded to accompany her body to the grave at Granada. There the pallbearers were obliged to swear that the corpse was genuine, on opening the leaden coffin. The empress, through humility, had asked before death that her body should not be embalmed, and seven days had passed since her body was placed in the coffin. When the duke took off the veil that covered her face he found her terribly changed and horrible to look upon. The body emitted such an unbearable odor that the spectators had to retire. Francis alone stood beside the coffin: "Is this the empress," he asked himself aloud, "who rejoiced all she looked on with her beauty and graciousness?" At sight of this sudden change Francis lost all care for the things of this fleeting world, and withdrew forever from the scenes of court life. But the emperor, who knew his worth, would not accept his resignation and appointed him to be governor of Catalonia. Francis fulfilled this duty till the death of his wife, when he gave up the world entirely and entered the Society of Jesus.

HUMILITY OF FRANCIS BORGIA.

St. Francis Borgia was a model of humility. When a member of his order he performed the humblest duties in the kitchen and stable. He always tried to serve his brethren. On one occasion, he carried to Madrid a plate of victuals to certain persons who had become poor and were ashamed to confess their poverty. He was met by his son Charles, Duke of Gondia, surrounded by a brilliant retinue. The saint placed the plate on his head and went forward to meet his son. The duke recognized his parent, dismounted from his horse, reverently greeted his father, and offered to carry the dish; this the holy man would not permit him to do, but carried it himself, and went on his way.

PATIENCE OF ST. FRANCIS.

St. Francis Borgia was once traveling with an old father who was afflicted with the asthma. They stayed over night in a lodging-house where there was only one bed to spare. Francis made the old man occupy the bed, while he himself laid on a bundle of straw on the floor. The sick father coughed all night long, and, without knowing it, spat on Francis, lying on the floor. When the father remarked his error in the morning, he was greatly excited. But Francis simply remarked; "Father, be not in the least troubled; you could not find in the room a more appropriate place to spit on than my face."

ST. PHILIP NERI AND THE STUDENT.

A young man once joyously remarked to St. Philip Neri that his parents had allowed him to study law. The saint listened, and then said: "And then?" The student answered: "Then I will be a lawyer." The saint continued: "And then?" "Then, I will bring complicated cases to a happy termination, and acquire fame and fortune." The saint continued: "And then?" "Then I will live a happy life and face old age joyously." The saint quietly repeated: "And then?" "Then," answered the student slowly, "I shall die." St. Philip raised his voice and asked in the most serious tone: "And then?" The young man made no answer, but walked away pondering on the words of the saint.

ST. PHILIP NERI, A FRIEND OF CHILDREN.

St. Philip Neri was a great friend of young people. He gave them presents, walked with them, participated in their amusements, and tried to add to their enjoyment. As soon as he had won their confidence, he talked to them on divine subjects. On the occasion of the carnival he was wont to bring his young followers to the seven principal churches of Rome. In his old age he even let them play ball close by his room. The people who lived in the house once objected to the noise made by the boys. The saint answered: "Do not be alarmed, children; play on and be happy. The only thing I ask of you is not to commit sin." On another occasion he said: "Provided you do not sin, you may do anything; you may even chop wood on my back."

HEROISM OF ST. FRANCIS SOLAN.

THREE hundred years ago St. Francis Solan set out as a missionary to the Indians of Peru. The ship in which he sailed was cast on a rock and immediately sprung a leak. The lifeboats were swung out. A number of people were taken in them, and St. Francis was asked to step in also. But he answered that he could not, amid such danger, desert his brethren. He exhorted, and comforted all around him, instructed the Moors who were on board in the truths of Christianity and baptized them. The ship suddenly broke in two, and a number of people on one portion of it were drowned. Solan was with those on the remaining half of the ship. When all uttered a cry of despair, he held out a crucifix, exhorted them to put their trust in God, and assured them that they would be saved. After three days and nights of anxiety and suffering, during which their courage was sustained by the exhortations of the saint, a ship came in sight. Even then Solan did not step on board until all the others had preceded him. To the astonishment of all, he had no sooner left the wreck than it disappeared beneath the waters.

PETER CLAVER, THE FRIEND OF THE NEGROES.

THE missionary Peter Claver lived, two hundred years ago, in Cartagena, South America. During his entire life he was the friend of the negroes who were landed at the place and sold as slaves. Every time a slave-ship arrived he went out, with wine, sweets and tobacco, to meet them, in order to win their confidence. He baptized the children who were born during the sea-voyage, and carried the sick from the ship on his shoulders. After the landing he would betake himself to the pen where the negroes were assembled, despite the horrible odor and stench of the place. He taught them how to make the sign of the cross, their prayers and the fundamental truths of Christianity. He crossed rivers and mountains, and penetrated jungles to reach the negroes. He implored their masters to treat them kindly, gave missions among them, and prepared the old and weak for death. He even saved a portion of his own food for distribution among them. He begged for them. He cleansed their wounds, prepared their beds, and attended those suffering from loathsome diseases, when no one else would attend them.

After the saint had spent thirty-six years in this charitable work in Cartagena and the surrounding country, his health gave out. He was scarcely dead when his room was plundered, so to speak, by the multitude who revered him, in order to secure some relic belonging to him. Pope Pius IX. placed him in the calendar of the saints in 1851. He is represented in Jesuit garb, with a crucifix in his hand and a negro standing beside him.

FOUNDING OF THE ORDER OF SISTERS OF CHARITY.

St. Vincent of Paul lived in Paris more than two hundred years ago. His heart was pained at sight of the misery of the poor and sick in that city. He saw that they could be assisted only through united effort. He therefore founded a union of young women, who, under his guidance, devoted their unpaid services to the sick. The sisters sought out the sick, begged for them from the rich, brought them food, did their washing, and attended to their wants night and day. With the aid of powerful benefactors, Vincent founded a mother house for the Sisterhood, and gave it a rule approved by the Pope. And from thence the Order of the Sisters of Charity has spread throughout the world.

ST. ALFONSUS LIGUORI.

THIS illustrious saint, founder of the Congregation of the Most Holy Redeemer, was born of a noble family near Naples, Italy, in 1696. He was placed by his pious parents under the patronage of the Blessed Virgin. His devotion to the Queen of Heaven during his after life is well known, as is evinced in his "Glories of Mary," and other works. A saying of his is that one truly devoted to Mary can never be lost.

The youth of Alfonsus was marked by gentleness and piety. His father intended him for the legal profession, and when little over twenty years of age he was a leading lawyer, and had been employed in many famous cases. In 1723 a case involving over 600,000 francs, between the Duke of Tuscany and another nobleman, came before the courts of Naples.

Alfonsus was retained on one side, which he presented with marvelous eloquence and legal acumen. But having overlooked by mere accident one document on which the whole case hinged, the opposing lawyer presented it, with the remark that it upset all the argument of Liguori. Alfonsus admitted the truth of his opponent's contention, and, with the exclamation, "World, I know thee now," left the courtroom and bade farewell to the law forever. He resolved to study for the holy ministry, and, after much opposition from his father, was ordained priest December 21, 1726. As a preacher he at once won fame, though he did not seek it. He devoted himself especially to the reclamation of sinners. The more hardened and wicked they were, the more gentle and fatherly was he towards them. He was sought for by sinners as incessantly and eagerly as he went in quest of them. He may, indeed, be called the Great Confessor. He once said: "I do not remember that I ever sent away a sinner without absolution." In 1732 he founded the Congregation known as the Redemptorists. By express command of the Pope he became Bishop of Agatta, which he would otherwise have refused. In 1775, by permission of the Pope, he resigned his bishopric and retired to his Congregation, where he died in 1787, in the ninety-sixth year of his age. The Congregation he has founded is ranked among the most efficient missionary organizations of the Catholic Church.

Thus a slight inadvertency caused this great saint to see the vanity of worldly greatness. Would that all youth would derive a similar lesson from their errors and disappointments.

LIVES OF SAINTS
CANONIZED BY
His Holiness Pope Leo XIII. in 1881.

ST. CLARE OF MONTEFALCO.

St. Clare was a native of a small Italian town (from which she took her name), and born in the thirteenth century. From her earliest infancy St. Clare devoted herself to the service of our Redeemer. She was blessed by visions apropos of a new monastery she established. She begged for the poor from house to house. She established a convent known as the Convent of the Holy Cross. Though but twenty-three years of age, Sister Clare was made abbess. She was especially devoted to the Passion of our Lord and to almsgiving. On one occasion our Saviour appeared to her bearing His cross, and said He wished to impress that cross in her heart. Subsequently, in her heart were found the various articles that were used in our dear Lord's crucifixion, and they remain even to this day, for after her death her heart was dissected, and in it was found the image of Jesus crucified, the pillar, the crown of thorns, the three nails, the lance and the reed with the sponge, all formed by flesh and veins. Her holiness increased, so that people from all parts came to beg the aid of her prayers. She was gifted with a prophetic spirit, and answered the most difficult questions put to her even by bishops. On the morning of the Feast of the Assumption of our Blessed Lady she sent for her spiritual director, and told him her life was drawing to a close. She then asked for the Holy Viaticum, and wished to be left alone, so that her thoughts might be fastened on her divine Saviour, and that nothing might draw them away. On the evening of the

17th of August, 1308, her attendants saw her face irradiated by a brilliant light coming from above. This light changed into the form of a globe and then disappeared, and with it departed the pure soul of St. Clare to meet her Creator.

ST. LAWRENCE OF BRINDISI.

ST. LAWRENCE was born in 1559, and was educated in a Franciscan convent. His parents died while he was yet young. In early life the saint joined the Capuchins. By diligent study he became a master of Hebrew, and was endowed with such eloquence that he was summoned by Pope Clement XIII. to Rome, to preach for the conversion of the Jews. His success was enormous, and his name soon became known through all Italy. He was successively administrator of many important positions, and when only thirty years of age was chosen Provincial of Tuscany, and three years later Provincial of Venice. The Turks, under Mahomet III., prepared to avenge their defeat at Lepanto. The saint, in order to avert from Christianity the great danger of a Turkish invasion, appealed to all the European governments, Catholic and Protestant, to meet the infidels, and soon had a powerful army in the field. Then, like a second Peter the Hermit, St. Lawrence stimulated the soldiers, so that they fought with great heroism and won a great victory over the overwhelming army of Turks. At one time the saint was borne into the thickest of the battle, and when pleaded with to remain at a distance replied heroically: "Here I am, and here I will stay until the fortune of the day is decided."

After his military service ended he was elected General of the Capuchins, the highest office of the Order, which he filled with great zeal and distinction. He died at Lisbon, July 22, 1616, and the Church under which he labored so successfully has recorded his numerous miracles.

ST. BENEDICT JOSEPH LABRE.

THIS recently canonized saint was born in France in 1748. His parents, on both sides, were pious. One of his distinguishing characteristics was his readiness of obedience. On one occasion, being unjustly charged with some fault he had not committed, in order to test his obedience, he declared his innocence, but when he was sent out to receive his punishment, he went in silence, preparing to receive it, when he was instead praised for his obedience. From his boyhood he served Mass, and always through his after life attended it with devotion as often as possible. He studied the classics with his uncle, a priest at Erin, France, but at the age of sixteen found his taste for knowledge lost, and he intended to join the rigorous Order of the Trappists. When applying at their monastery he was refused admittance. The same happened to him on seeking admission to five other monasteries. He traveled to all these distant places, many hundred miles, always on foot, begging his meals as he went along. After these trials, he saw plainly that God's holy will was for him to make pilgrimages to the holy places in Europe.

Clothed in rags tied by knotted ropes, he made eleven journeys to the Holy House of Loretto, besides many to other shrines. In Lent of 1783 he dropped exhausted in one of the streets in Rome, and died April 16th as the Angelus was rung, at 8 o'clock in the evening, when his pilgrimages were forever ended. A Protestant minister of Boston, on the occasion of his canonization, undertook to investigate his miracles, was convinced of their truth, and became a Catholic and a priest.

ST. JOHN BAPTIST DE ROSSI.

St. John Baptist de Rossi was born at Voltagio, a little town in Italy, in 1698. From early childhood he was distinguished for his piety and purity. At the age of ten years he was adopted by a wealthy family of Genoa as their son. When a boy of thirteen years he visited the Roman college, where he was a model for his fellow-students. Having overtaxed his strength in his studies as well as in leading an austere life, his health began to fail, and although he had received tonsure already, he was obliged to interrupt his course. Later he joined a comparatively lighter course, and was ordained a priest at the age of twenty-three. From the beginning of his priesthood he took active interest in the young students who flocked to Rome from all parts of the world, organizing special services for them in church, preaching sermons to them suited to their state of life, and practically teaching them the works of charity by his own example. Another class of men whom he endeavored to bring back to a good Christian life were the ignorant and depraved drovers and cattlemen who frequented the market-places of the city of Rome. In 1737 he became Canon of Santa Maria in Cosmedin. Throughout his whole life his devotion to the poor and ignorant was remarkable, sacrificing for them his talent, time and health. The latter was ruined at last by endless labor and severe penance, and on May 23, 1764, a stroke of apoplexy ended his precious life. After his death many miracles bore witness to his holiness.

AMERICAN SAINTS,
RECENTLY PLACED IN THE PROPER
FOR THE UNITED STATES,
AT THE PETITION OF THE
Third Plenary Council of Baltimore.

St. Philip of Jesus, martyr, was a native of Mexico, and, therefore, with the exception of St. Rose of Lima, is the only saint born on American soil. Intended by his parents for the Church, he refused to adopt a religious life, and went in a mercantile capacity on a voyage to the Philippine Islands. While there he changed his mind, and entered the Franciscan Order in 1594. Two years subsequently he sailed for his native country, but the frail vessel was tossed about by storms, and wrecked on the coast of Japan. Having been captured by the authorities, who hated the Christian name, he, with twenty-five companions, were put to death by crucifixion, a death Friar Philip earnestly desired. Having wrought many miracles, which were duly attested, he was canonized, under the title of St. Philip of Jesus, by our late Holy Father Pope Pius IX.

ST. TURRIBIUS, Archbishop of Lima, and ST. FRANCIS SOLANO, are likewise regarded as American saints, though both were born in Spain. But most of their lives and all their labors may be claimed by America. The former was from his youth noted for his piety and sweetness of manner. He studied assiduously, and soon became distinguished for his learning as well as for his piety. Though a layman, King Philip of Spain wrote to the Holy Father begging to have Turribius Mogrobejo appointed Archbishop of Lima. His Holiness consented. When informed of the event, Turribius was amazed, and did not credit the intelligence; but when he was told that the Holy Father desired him to prepare to receive Holy Orders, he consented. Entering on his duties as Archbishop of Lima in 1587, he soon changed the religious character of his immense diocese. He passed more than a dozen years in making visitations among his flock, extirpating vice, reclaiming the erring, framing new ecclesiastical laws, and doing good everywhere. He died in 1666, and was canonized by Pope Benedict XIII. in 1726.

St. Francis Solano, a Spaniard, as already mentioned, sailed for Peru in 1589. When near the South American shore the vessel was cast on the rocks, and though requested by the captain to escape, with a few others he courageously refused the offer. He remained on the stranded vessel for three days, comforting and exhorting the terrified passengers, who were mostly negro slaves, until at last all were rescued. He changed the character of Lima by his fervent exhortations, and devoted much of his life, amid grave hardships, to the conversion of the Indians, nine thousand of whom he baptized. He died in the year 1610, and was canonized by Benedict XIII. in 1726.

These three saints have lately been placed in the Proper for the United States at the request of the Third Plenary Council of Baltimore.

www.ingramcontent.com/pod-product-compliance
Lightning Source LLC
Chambersburg PA
CBHW020857230426
43666CB00008B/1220